Sainsbury's

·RECIPE·LIBRARY·

FISH & SHELLFISH

Sainsbury's

·RECIPE·LIBRARY·

FISH & SHELLFISH

Mary Cadogan

CONTENTS

Published exclusively for J Sainsbury plc
Stamford House Stamford Street London SE1 9LL
by Martin Books
Simon & Schuster International Group
Fitzwilliam House 32 Trumpington Street
Cambridge CB2 1QY

ISBN 0 85941 498 1
First published 1987
Second impression 1990

Printed and bound in Italy by Arnoldo Mondadori Editore

INTRODUCTION

Fish can fit so appropriately into every occasion, it is amazing we don't eat more of it. It is quick-cooking, relatively inexpensive and very tasty, with the added advantage of being low in fat. This healthy food has been left out of the limelight far too long and I hope these recipes will help to give it a starring role in your cooking.

Many of you may be unsure of how to buy, cook and present fish. Read on and you will find out how simple it is. Fish doesn't like fuss. The simplest recipes are almost always the most successful. Good news for those in a hurry—and who isn't these days?

Fish has the added attraction of versatility. Look at your fish counter and check on the varieties available, all of which can be cooked in countless ways, so you need never grow tired of fish. Don't forget that you can ask at the fish counter for the meat to be removed from a lobster or crab, and you can have fish scaled, gutted or filleted on request. However, if you do have to scale, gut or fillet a fish, follow the step-by-step instructions on pages 6–7 and, armed with a sharp knife, you will find it really isn't so difficult.

For a special meal it is a good idea either to order the fish in advance, particularly salmon or bass, or plan the menu around the best fish available that day. You will find I have given alternatives for many recipes.

To make menu-planning easier, I have grouped the recipes into 4 chapters, according to the occasion:

Starters and Cocktail Snacks includes soups such as Mediterranean-style Fish Soup, liberally laced with garlic and wine; elegant dishes such as Lobster, Paw-Paw and Avocado Salad; and the light and delicate flavours of Smoked Trout and Watercress Pâté and Salmon and Lettuce Pinwheels—ideal appetizers to serve with drinks.

Easy Suppers offers a wealth of ideas when time and money are not on your side. Baked Fish Pasta can be made ahead of time if needed, and Caribbean Cod Stew is assembled in minutes, using a few choice ingredients. Ace Fish Pie is one the whole family will love.

Light Dishes features recipes which can be served as a substantial starter or light main meal. Many of them are special enough for entertaining: try Scallops with Black Bean Sauce or Lemon Sole Fillets with Prawn and Chervil Sauce. For light lunches choose from Mussel and Leek Tarts, Jacket Potatoes with Potted Shrimps or Grilled Plaice with Crispy Bacon.

Entertaining, the final chapter, shows what a good choice fish is for special occasions: it fits well with other courses without being too filling. A whole baked fish such as the snapper in Janice's Scobeche or Irish Baked Salmon always looks spectacular, needs little attention, and leaves you free to be with your guests. For convenience, the batter and sauce for the quick-cooking Tempura can be prepared ahead and spicy King Prawns Creole can be completely made in advance and reheated for serving.

BUYING AND STORING FISH AND SHELLFISH
As fish is very perishable it must be bought and eaten when it is absolutely fresh. You can recognize fresh whole fish by their shiny moist skin, pink gills and bright, not sunken, eyes.

To touch, fresh fish will feel soft, but not springy. The smell should be clean and pleasant, not fishy or overpowering. Fish fillets and steaks will have translucent, milky flesh, with no sign of dryness, when fresh.

Shellfish such as lobsters, crabs and prawns, are generally sold cooked, or cooked and frozen, as they deteriorate rapidly; raw prawns and shrimps in their shells are sometimes available, in which case they are deep grey in colour —they turn the familiar pink colour on cooking. Scallops are most commonly available, either fresh or frozen, already removed from their shells and cleaned, ready for cooking. Both fish and shellfish are best eaten on the day they are bought, but they can be kept for up to 24 hours in the refrigerator, loosely-wrapped in foil.

Some fresh fish is also available in specially sealed packets to prolong its storage life. Known as CAP (Controlled Atmosphere Packaged) fish, this can be kept for a few days in the refrigerator—ideal when you need to shop in advance.

TO GUT A ROUND FISH (such as trout, herring, mackerel etc.)
1. Place the fish on several layers of kitchen paper. Cut off the fins and trim the tail if you like.
2. Using sharp scissors, cut down the belly from the head to the vent. Scrape out the entrails, then run the point of a knife down either side of the backbone to remove the blood.
3. Scrape out any black skin from the flesh. Rinse the fish under running cold water, then pat dry with kitchen paper.

TO GUT A FLAT FISH (such as plaice, sole etc.)
1. Place the fish on several layers of kitchen paper. Cut off the fins and trim the tail if you like. Using a sharp pointed knife, make a small slit on the dark skin just below the head.
2. Scrape out the entrails, which are quite easy to locate and only occupy a small area.
3. Rinse the fish under running cold water, then pat dry with kitchen paper.

TO SCALE A FISH
Some fish, such as red mullet and sea bass, have hard scales which need to be removed before the fish is cooked. It is a good idea to cover the work surface with newspaper before you start, because the scales fly in all directions.
1. Place the fish on several layers of kitchen paper, or on the draining board. Hold the fish by the tail using a folded piece of kitchen paper to give a good grip.
2. Using the back of a large knife, scrape towards the head to remove the scales on both sides of the fish. Rinse the knife occasionally to discard scales.
3. Rinse the fish and run a hand over the skin to check all the scales are removed.

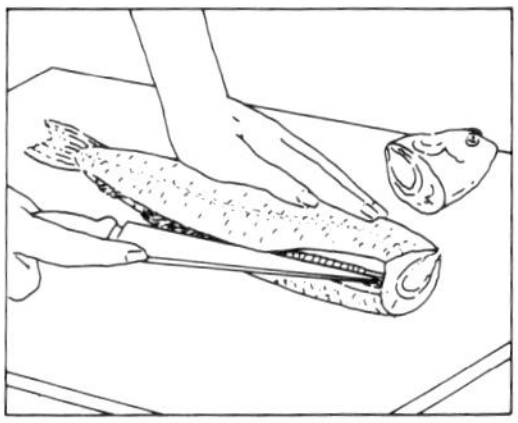

Fig i

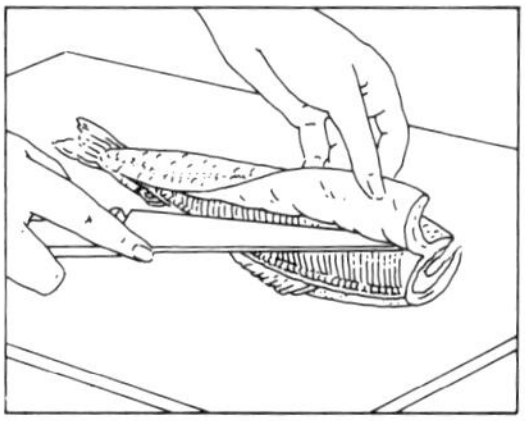

Fig ii

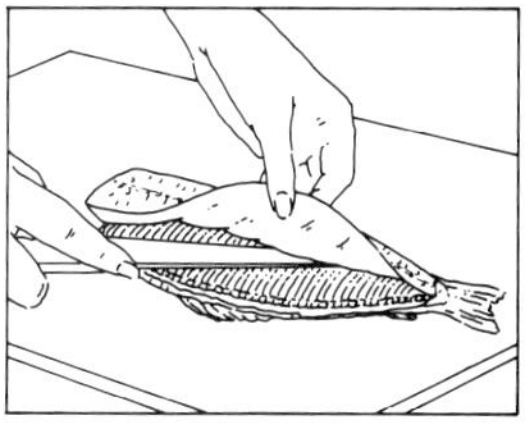

Fig iii

TO FILLET A ROUND FISH (such as trout, herring, mackerel etc.)

1. Remove the head, gut and rinse the fish. Cut the fish all along the backbone (Fig i).
2. Holding the knife at an angle and keeping it close to the bones, ease the upper fillet away (Fig ii).
3. Turn the fish over and cut the second fillet away from the bones (Fig iii).

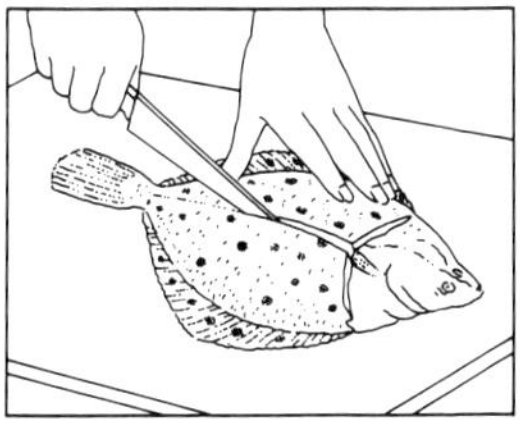

Fig i

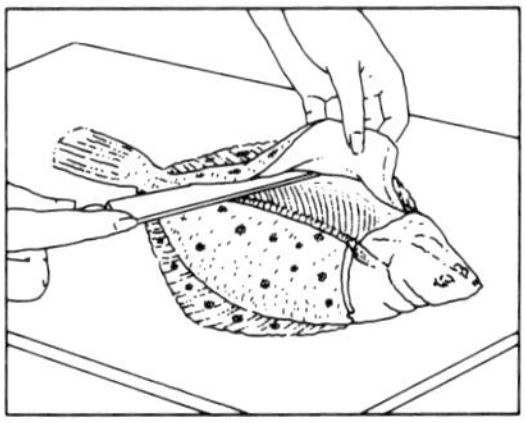

Fig ii

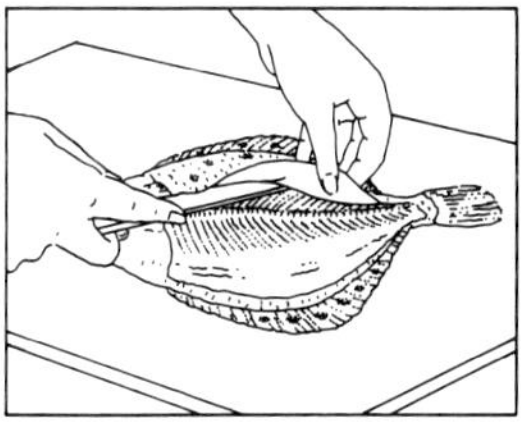

Fig iii

TO FILLET A FLAT FISH (such as plaice, sole etc.)

1. Place the fish on a board with the head away from you. Using a sharp knife, gut the fish, then cut down the backbone from the head to the tail (Fig i).
2. To remove one fillet, hold your knife at an angle along the backbone, then work the flesh away from the bones towards one edge of the fish, using long strokes of the knife. Keep the knife flat against the bones and turn the flesh back with your other hand as you work (Fig ii).
3. Turn the fish around with the head facing you and remove the second fillet in the same way (Fig iii).
4. Turn the fish over and remove the 2 fillets from the other side in the same way. Use the bones and head to make fish stock.

TO SKIN A FISH FILLET

1. Place the fish fillet, skin side down, on a board with the tail end towards you. Using a large sharp knife, cut a little flesh away from the skin at the tail end.
2. Dip your fingers in salt to give a good grip and hold the skin with one hand. Slip the knife between the flesh and skin, keeping it almost flat against the skin.
3. Separate the flesh from the skin using a sawing action and pressing down firmly with the knife.

When using frozen fish, remove the skin while still frozen. It can be peeled off easily with the fingers. Pick up one corner of the skin, then pull the skin off sharply in one piece.

TO SKIN A FLAT FISH (such as plaice, sole, etc.)
1. Lay the fish dark skin uppermost on a board. Make a cut across the skin at the tail end.
2. Hold the tail firmly with kitchen paper and pull the skin off the fish in one movement towards the head.
3. Turn the fish over and repeat with the white side, unless you prefer to remove the dark skin only.

TO CLEAN MUSSELS
1. Check the mussels are firmly closed. Any that are open should be sharply tapped. They will close if they are alive. Any dead ones that remain open must be discarded.
2. Using a small strong knife, scrape the shells under running cold water to remove anything clinging to them. Pull off the beard (the hairy strands attached to the hinge of the shell).
3. Wash the mussels in several changes of water and cook them on the day of purchase.

FISH STOCK
It is very worthwhile making a simple stock—you can have the pot simmering while you prepare your fish recipe.

Wash the head, bones and skin of a filleted fish, together with any prawn shells, and place in a pan with 1.2 litres (2 pints) water, 6 peppercorns, 1 clove, 1 small onion, quartered, 1 celery stick, chopped, 1 bay leaf, a few sprigs of parsley and dill, and salt to taste. Bring slowly to the boil, skimming off any scum with a slotted spoon.

Partially cover and simmer for 20 minutes, skimming if necessary. Strain the stock through a fine sieve lined with kitchen paper, and cool quickly.

Freeze in ice cube trays or small containers as many recipes need just a little stock for moistening or flavouring sauces etc.

COOKING FISH AND SHELLFISH
As fish is naturally tender it only needs to be cooked for a short time, unlike many cuts of meat. However the type of fish should be matched carefully to the cooking method.

Poaching: Not to be confused with boiling. The fish is cooked in barely simmering liquid which may be water, wine, milk or stock, often flavoured with herbs, lemon and aromatic vegetables. The cooking liquid can then be reduced to form the basis of a sauce. Smoked fish is good poached in a milk and water mixture to help rid it of any saltiness. The liquid for poaching should always be kept to a minimum to avoid loss of flavour. Whole large fish such as salmon or bass need to be cooked in a special long pan to keep them intact. If you don't have one, the fish can be baked in foil.

Steaming: Fish can be steamed in a special perforated steamer, on a rack inside a wok or fish kettle, or on a covered heatproof plate over a pan of boiling water. Steaming helps retain moisture and flavour and is particularly good for fine-flavoured fish such as plaice or sole. Shellfish, such as mussels and cockles, are usually steamed in their own juices.

Stewing and Braising: These are simply an extension of poaching where fish is concerned, as it is rarely necessary to prolong the cooking time to tenderize the fish. Fish stews, soups and chowders are included here. In a fish stew, an assortment of fish is often cooked gently in liquid with the addition of vegetables, herbs, oil and garlic. In this way a lovely rich juice is formed, which is best mopped up with fresh crusty bread.

Baking: Fish cooked in the oven is usually covered in some way to prevent it from drying out. A little liquid in the form of water, wine or stock is poured over the fish and used for basting during cooking.

Another way of protecting the fish is by wrapping it in a foil or paper parcel. Seasonings, butter, stuffings etc., are added along with a little liquid to keep the fish moist.

Frying: Most fish can be shallow- or deep-fried, but as the temperatures are so high it is often best to give it a protective coating. This could be seasoned flour, oatmeal, egg and crumbs or batter. As fish is so tender, the cooking time is very brief so timing is crucial. Use blended vegetable oil for deep-frying as it has a neutral flavour and is inexpensive; sunflower oil or groundnut oil should be used for stir-frying as they do not burn easily.

Grilling and Barbecuing: Grilling is the simplest cooking method and one suited to a wide range of fish. Oily fish, such as mackerel, are ideal for grilling. Slash them on both sides of the skin to ensure even cooking. The fish can first be seasoned with nothing more than a few herb sprigs, salt, pepper and a squeeze of lemon. Flat fish, such as sole or plaice, can be grilled whole and should be brushed with melted butter or oil to keep them moist. Whole fish, such as trout and mullet, are particularly good grilled or barbecued. They can be wrapped in vine leaves for flavour and to protect them from the searing heat. Shellfish, such as halved lobster, may be grilled after brushing with oil or melted butter. Mediterranean prawns, scallops or mussels threaded onto skewers are good for the barbecue.

Fish to be grilled or barbecued can be marinated to add extra flavour and keep the flesh moist during cooking. A simple marinade consists of oil and lemon juice or wine vinegar flavoured with onion, garlic, seasonings and herbs; choose from thyme, rosemary, tarragon, mint, crushed juniper berries, chillies. Leave the fish in the marinade for 1–2 hours and then use the marinade for basting the fish during cooking.

NOTES

Ingredients are given in both metric and imperial measures. Use either set of quantities but not a mixture of both in any one recipe.

All spoon measurements are level:
1 tablespoon = one 15 ml spoon
1 teaspoon = one 5 ml spoon.

Ovens should be preheated to the temperature specified.

Freshly ground black pepper is intended where pepper is listed.

Fresh herbs are used unless otherwise stated. If unobtainable, dried herbs can be substituted in cooked dishes but halve the quantities.

Eggs are standard size 3 unless otherwise stated.

BAKED CRAB

Have the crabs prepared at the fish counter: ask for the edible meat to be piled back into the shells, and retain the small legs for garnish if you wish.

4 small cooked crabs, prepared
1 small onion, grated
1 green chilli, seeded and chopped finely
2 tablespoons lime juice
2 tablespoons snipped chives
25 g (1 oz) butter, melted
25 g (1 oz) wholemeal breadcrumbs
salt and pepper to taste
TO GARNISH:
lime or lemon wedges
parsley sprigs

Serves 4
Preparation time:
20 minutes
Cooking time:
20 minutes
Freezing:
Recommended

1. Remove the crab meat from the shells and place in a bowl with the onion, chilli, lime juice, chives and butter. Season with pepper, and salt if necessary, and mix well.
2. Pile back into the shells and sprinkle with the breadcrumbs. Cook in a preheated oven, 190°C/375°F/Gas Mark 5, for 20 minutes, until the topping is golden brown. Serve hot, garnished with lime or lemon wedges and parsley.

SPICED MELON WITH PRAWNS

This simple dish makes a refreshing starter and is a perfect prelude to a rich or spicy meal.

1 Galia or Cantaloupe melon
175 g (6 oz) peeled prawns (thawed if frozen)
juice of 2 limes
½ teaspoon chilli powder
salt and pepper to taste

Serves 4
Preparation time:
15 minutes, plus chilling
Freezing:
Not recommended

1. Cut the melon in half and discard the seeds. Cut the flesh into cubes, or balls using a melon baller, and place in a bowl with the prawns. Mix well.
2. Add the lime juice, chilli powder, a generous amount of pepper and a little salt. Mix well, cover and chill for 2 hours.
3. Transfer to individual dishes to serve.

POTTED MACKEREL WITH CIDER

Moist-fleshed mackerel takes very kindly to potting and will keep for two days in the refrigerator.

2 mackerel, each weighing about 350 g (12 oz), gutted and heads removed
300 ml (½ pint) dry cider
½ teaspoon ground mace
1 tablespoon freshly squeezed orange juice
¼ teaspoon chilli powder
125 g (4 oz) butter, melted
salt and pepper to taste
TO GARNISH:
orange slices
salad leaves
dill sprigs

Serves 4–6
Preparation time: 20 minutes, plus chilling
Cooking time: 30 minutes
Freezing: Recommended

1. Place the mackerel in a shallow ovenproof dish and pour over the cider. Cover with foil and cook in a preheated oven, 190°C/375°F/Gas Mark 5, for 30 minutes, until tender. Remove from the dish with a fish slice and leave until cool enough to handle; reserve the cider.
2. Remove the skin and bones from the fish. Flake the flesh and mix with about 2 tablespoons of the reserved cider, the mace, orange juice, chilli powder, and salt and pepper. Stir in half of the butter and mix well.
3. Pack the mixture into a small serving dish and smooth the top. Pour over the remaining butter and chill overnight or for at least 4 hours.
4. Place scoops of the potted mackerel on individual plates and garnish with orange slices, salad leaves and dill sprigs. Serve with toasted granary bread.

DEEP-FRIED PLAICE WITH SKORDALIA

Skordalia is a wonderful Greek garlic and almond sauce. It is perfect with any fried fish, but you need to be a garlic lover to appreciate it. You have been warned!

50 g (2 oz) ground almonds
4 tablespoons white wine vinegar
3 cloves garlic, crushed
125 ml (4 fl oz) olive oil
4 plaice fillets, each weighing about 175 g (6 oz), skinned
175 g (6 oz) self-raising flour
1 teaspoon paprika
250 ml (8 fl oz) water
salt and pepper to taste
oil for deep-frying
frisé or watercress sprigs to garnish

1. Place the ground almonds, vinegar, garlic, 2 tablespoons water, and salt and pepper in a blender or food processor and work together until well mixed. With the machine running, gradually add the olive oil until a creamy sauce forms; add a little more water if it appears too thick. Turn into a small dish and chill for at least 1 hour.
2. Cut the plaice crossways into 2 cm (¾ inch) wide strips. Sift the flour, paprika and a little salt into a bowl. Gradually add the water, beating constantly, to form a smooth batter.
3. Add the plaice strips to the batter and toss until evenly coated. Remove with a fork, discarding any excess batter. Deep-fry in hot oil, in batches if necessary, for 2–3 minutes, until crisp and golden; drain on kitchen paper.
4. Serve on warmed individual plates, garnished with frisé or watercress, and hand the skordalia separately.

Serves 4
Preparation time:
30 minutes, plus chilling
Cooking time:
2–3 minutes per batch
Freezing:
Not recommended

SMOKED TROUT AND WATERCRESS PÂTÉ

This pink and green dappled pâté looks very pretty served with a basket of crudités and warm toast. It should not be too smooth, so take care not to over process it.

1 smoked trout, weighing about 350 g (12 oz)
1 bunch watercress
3 tablespoons freshly squeezed orange juice
113 g (4 oz) curd cheese
50 g (2 oz) butter, melted
salt and pepper to taste
orange and cucumber slices to garnish

Serves 4–6
Preparation time: 25 minutes
Freezing: Not recommended

1. Remove the skin and bones from the trout. Break the fish into several pieces, place in a blender or food processor and work until fairly smooth.
2. Remove the tough stalks from the watercress. Add the leaves to the blender or processor and work until finely chopped. Transfer to a mixing bowl.
3. Stir in the remaining ingredients. Press into a small dish and smooth the top. Chill until required, then serve on individual plates, garnished with orange and cucumber.

SEAFOOD SALAD WITH PINK GRAPEFRUIT

75 g (3 oz) mangetouts
1 ruby red grapefruit
1 large tomato, skinned and seeded
2 tablespoons olive oil
1 teaspoon chopped mixed herbs
1 teaspoon clear honey
3 tablespoons natural set yogurt
selection of salad leaves
12–16 cooked peeled Mediterranean prawns
few cooked scallops, quartered
salt and pepper to taste

1. Cook the mangetouts for 1 minute in boiling salted water. Drain quickly, then cool under running cold water.
2. Peel the grapefruit over a bowl to catch the juices. Remove all the white pith, then cut down between the membranes into segments. Set aside.
3. Place the tomato, oil, herbs, honey, yogurt, and salt and pepper in a blender or food processor and work together until smooth. Add 1 tablespoon of the grapefruit juice.
4. Arrange the salad leaves on 4 individual plates. Top with the prawns, scallops if using, mangetouts and grapefruit and drizzle over the dressing to serve.

Serves 4
Preparation time:
25 minutes
Freezing:
Not recommended

TUNA, BEAN AND POTATO SALAD

350 g (12 oz) new potatoes
198 g (7 oz) can tuna, drained and flaked
432 g (15¼ oz) can borlotti beans, drained
2 shallots or small onions, sliced thinly
shredded lettuce to serve

FOR THE DRESSING:
1 clove garlic, chopped
1 teaspoon Dijon mustard
2 tablespoons wine vinegar
4 tablespoons olive oil
1 tablespoon chopped parsley
salt and pepper to taste

Serves 4
Preparation time: 15 minutes
Cooking time: About 20 minutes
Freezing: Not recommended

1. Cook the potatoes in boiling salted water for about 20 minutes, until tender, drain and leave to cool. Cut into quarters if they are large and place in a bowl.
2. Add the tuna, beans and shallots or onions; mix lightly.
3. Place the dressing ingredients in a screw-top jar and shake well to mix. Pour over the salad and mix lightly.
4. Serve on shredded lettuce with warm granary bread.

CARIBBEAN COD AND AVOCADO SALAD

350 g (12 oz) cod fillet
6 peppercorns
1 tablespoon white wine vinegar
1 bay leaf
5 cm (2 inch) piece cucumber, peeled and sliced
2 tomatoes, skinned and sliced
1 green chilli, seeded and chopped finely
1 ripe avocado

FOR THE DRESSING:
2 tablespoons lime juice
3 tablespoons sunflower oil
1 teaspoon Dijon mustard
2 tablespoons chopped parsley
salt and pepper to taste

Serves 4
Preparation time: 20 minutes
Cooking time: 12–15 minutes
Freezing: Not recommended

1. Place the cod, peppercorns, vinegar and bay leaf in a pan and cover with water. Bring to the boil, then cover and cook gently for 12–15 minutes, until the fish is tender. Remove carefully with a fish slice, cool slightly, then skin and flake the fish. Leave to cool.
2. Mix together the fish, cucumber, tomatoes and chilli.
3. Peel and stone the avocado and chop the flesh. Add to the fish mixture and mix lightly.
4. Place the dressing ingredients in a screw-top jar and shake well to mix. Pour over the salad and toss lightly. Serve immediately, with warm bread.

SPICED PRAWN SALAD

1 tablespoon wine vinegar
1 teaspoon coarse-grain mustard
½ teaspoon paprika
½ teaspoon chilli powder
2 tablespoons sunflower oil
2 tablespoons finely chopped spring onions
1 celery stick, chopped finely
175 g (6 oz) peeled prawns (thawed if frozen)
½ avocado
shredded lettuce or frisé (curly endive)

Serves 4
Preparation time: 15 minutes, plus marinating
Freezing: Not recommended

1. Place the vinegar, mustard, paprika and chilli powder in a bowl, mix well, then gradually stir in the oil until slightly thickened. Add the spring onions, celery and prawns and mix well. Leave to marinate for about 30 minutes, if possible.
2. Peel and chop the avocado.
3. Divide the lettuce or frisé and avocado between 4 individual dishes and spoon the prawn mixture over the top to serve.

LOBSTER, PAW-PAW AND AVOCADO SALAD

Have the lobster halved and the meat removed at the fish counter.

1 cooked lobster, weighing about 1 kg (2 lb)
1 paw-paw
1 avocado
crisp lettuce leaves
1 tablespoon tarragon vinegar
4 tablespoons olive oil
salt and pepper to taste
chervil sprigs to garnish

Serves 4
Preparation time: 20 minutes
Freezing: Not recommended

1. Remove all the meat from the lobster, including the claws. Slice the tail meat and dice the remainder.
2. Cut the paw-paw in half. Remove the seeds and peel. Thinly slice one half and reserve the other half.
3. Peel, stone and slice the avocado.
4. Arrange the lettuce on 4 individual plates. Arrange a fan of alternate paw-paw and avocado slices on each plate. Divide the lobster between the plates.
5. Chop the reserved paw-paw, place in a blender or food processor with the vinegar, oil, and salt and pepper and work together until smooth. Drizzle a little sauce over each salad and garnish with chervil to serve.

MUSSEL CHOWDER

150 ml (¼ pint) white wine
1.2 litres (2 pints) fresh mussels, cleaned (see page 8)
4 rashers streaky bacon, derinded and chopped
25 g (1 oz) butter
1 onion, chopped
1 leek, shredded
1 celery stick, chopped
500 g (1 lb) potatoes, cubed
300 ml (½ pint) milk
142 ml (5 fl oz) carton single cream
2 tablespoons chopped parsley
salt and pepper to taste

Serves 4–6
Preparation time: 25 minutes
Cooking time: 30 minutes
Freezing: Not recommended

1. Bring the wine and 300 ml (½ pint) water to the boil in a large pan. Add the mussels, and salt and pepper, cover tightly and cook for about 5 minutes, until the shells have opened. Drain, reserving the liquid, and discard any mussels that have not opened. Remove the mussels from their shells.
2. Place the bacon in the pan and heat gently until the fat runs. Add the butter, onion, leek and celery and fry for 5 minutes. Add the potatoes and reserved liquid, bring to the boil, then cover and simmer for 20 minutes, until the potatoes are tender.
3. Add the mussels, milk, cream, parsley, and salt and pepper and heat through for about 5 minutes. Serve piping hot, with crusty bread.

FISH SOUP

This country-style soup is rich and substantial. Serve a light main course after it or have it as a meal in itself, with plenty of bread to mop up the juices.

2 tablespoons olive oil
2 cloves garlic, crushed
1 Spanish onion, chopped
2 courgettes, sliced
1 bay leaf
1 bouquet garni
150 ml (¼ pint) cider or dry white wine
450 ml (¾ pint) water or fish stock
250 g (8 oz) ripe tomatoes, skinned and chopped
1 red mullet or trout, weighing about 350 g (12 oz), gutted and scaled
2 plaice fillets, skinned
250 g (8 oz) smoked cod or haddock fillet, skinned and cubed
125 g (4 oz) peeled prawns (thawed if frozen)
salt and pepper to taste

1. Heat the oil in a large saucepan, add the garlic and onion and fry until softened. Add the courgettes and turn in the oil to coat.
2. Add the bay leaf, bouquet garni, cider or wine, water or stock, tomatoes, and salt and pepper. Bring to the boil, stirring well, then cover and simmer for 20 minutes.
3. Remove the head from the mullet or trout and cut the fish into steaks through the bone. Cut each plaice fillet lengthways into 4 strips. Add both to the soup with the cod or haddock, cover and cook for 10 minutes. Add the prawns and cook for 5 minutes. Serve immediately.

Serves 4–6
Preparation time:
30 minutes
Cooking time:
35 minutes
Freezing:
Recommended

OPEN SANDWICHES

A selection of beautifully garnished open sandwiches looks very inviting. They are simple to prepare, too, with a few well-chosen ingredients.

The bread should be firm, preferably granary, rye or wholemeal; the crusts may be removed if you wish. Spread the butter evenly to the edges to provide a good anchor for the toppings, which must be very generous. The sandwich is easiest eaten with a knife and fork.

There is no recipe as such for the toppings—they can be as flexible as you like—but here are a few ideas to give you a start.

HERRING AND APPLE. Cover the bread with lettuce. Cut a rollmop herring into strips. Quarter, core and slice a red dessert apple. Arrange the herring and apple alternately on the lettuce. Mix some mustard with a little yogurt or soured cream and spoon on top. Sprinkle with capers and garnish with a dill sprig.

SALMON AND CAVIAR. Cover the bread with frisé (curly endive) and drape a couple of slices of smoked salmon over the top. Add a spoonful of mayonnaise and top with red or black caviar, or a mixture. Garnish with lemon and cucumber slices.

CRAB AND SALAD. Cover the bread with watercress and shredded lettuce. Grate a courgette and a carrot, mix together and moisten with a little French dressing. Moisten some crab meat with mayonnaise and season with a pinch of chilli powder, salt and pepper. Place alternate rows of crab and salad diagonally over the leaves. Garnish with a radish.

SALMON AND LETTUCE PINWHEELS

These tasty cocktail snacks are quick to prepare and can be made well in advance. If you prefer, serve on 4 individual plates as a starter.

175 g (6 oz) smoked salmon
1 tablespoon milk
62.5 g (2.2 oz) packet soft cheese with garlic and herbs
few lettuce leaves

Makes about 30
Preparation time: 10 minutes, plus chilling
Freezing: Not recommended

1. Place the salmon on a board, overlapping the slices to make 2 oblong shapes about 10 × 15 cm (4 × 6 inches).
2. Beat together the milk and cheese and spread evenly over the salmon. Cover with lettuce, trimming as necessary, and press down lightly. Roll up from one long edge, place on a plate and chill for 1–2 hours, until firm.
3. Cut the rolls into slices about 1 cm (½ inch) thick, then skewer each through the centre with a cocktail stick.

SESAME PRAWN TOASTS

This Chinese speciality makes a wonderful snack or starter. It can be assembled early in the day, ready for deep-frying.

350 g (12 oz) raw prawns, peeled and chopped roughly
½ teaspoon salt
1 egg white
2 spring onions, chopped finely
2 teaspoons light soy sauce
1 teaspoon grated fresh root ginger
5 thin slices day-old bread, crusts removed, cut into quarters
2 tablespoons sesame seeds
oil for deep-frying
spring onion to garnish

Makes 20
Preparation time: 15 minutes
Cooking time: 4–5 minutes per batch
Freezing: Not recommended

1. Place the prawns, salt, egg white, spring onions, soy sauce and ginger in a blender or food processor and work together until fairly smooth and well mixed.
2. Spread the mixture generously over each piece of bread, smoothing it into a neat mound. Sprinkle with the sesame seeds.
3. Deep-fry the toasts in batches, prawn side down, in hot oil, for 4–5 minutes, turning once, until golden brown. Drain well on kitchen paper. Serve piping hot.

SMOKED TROUT IN PASTRY BOATS

You can make the pastry cases and tomato sauce in advance, but don't assemble them until about 1 hour before serving.

250 g (8 oz) plain flour
125 g (4 oz) butter or margarine
25 g (1 oz) Parmesan cheese, grated
1 teaspoon mustard powder
2 tablespoons water
250 g (8 oz) ripe tomatoes, chopped
1 bay leaf
1 teaspoon paprika
1 small onion, chopped
500 g (1 lb) smoked trout fillets
142 ml (5 fl oz) carton double cream, whipped
salt and pepper to taste
TO GARNISH:
dill sprigs
lemon slices, quartered

1. Sift the flour into a bowl and rub in the fat until the mixture resembles fine breadcrumbs. Stir in the cheese and mustard, then mix to a firm dough with the water.

2. Turn onto a lightly floured board and knead until smooth, then roll out thinly and use to line 20 boat-shaped tins or bun tins. Prick the bases with a fork, then bake in a preheated oven, 200°C/400°F/Gas Mark 6, for 12–15 minutes, until golden brown. Cool on a wire rack.
3. Meanwhile, place the tomatoes, bay leaf, paprika, onion, and salt and pepper in a small pan. Bring to the boil, then simmer, uncovered, for 7–10 minutes, until thickened. Press through a sieve and leave until cold.
4. Just before serving, place a small piece of trout in each pastry case, cutting to fit. Fold the cream into the tomato sauce and spoon a little into each pastry case. Garnish with dill sprigs and lemon.

Makes 20
Preparation time:
30 minutes
Cooking time:
12–15 minutes
Freezing:
Not recommended

MACKEREL WITH LIME AND ONION

2 limes
4 mackerel, each weighing 250 g (8 oz), gutted and filleted
6 spring onions, chopped
few dill sprigs
150 ml (1/4 pint) dry cider
2 bay leaves
salt and pepper to taste

Serves 4
Preparation time:
10 minutes
Cooking time:
30–40 minutes
Freezing:
Not recommended

1. Peel the limes, discarding all pith, then slice the fruit thinly.
2. Arrange the lime, spring onions and dill over one half of each fish. Sprinkle with salt and pepper, place the other fish half on top and secure with wooden cocktail sticks, if necessary.
3. Place in a greased baking dish, pour over the cider and add the bay leaves. Cover with foil and cook in a preheated oven, 180°C/350°F/Gas Mark 4, for 30–40 minutes, until tender. Serve hot, with a side salad.

HADDOCK AND VEGETABLE HOTPOT

1 tablespoon oil
1 onion, sliced thinly
1 green pepper, cored, seeded and sliced
2 Beefsteak tomatoes, skinned and chopped
1 teaspoon chopped oregano
500 g (1 lb) potatoes, cubed
2 teaspoons tomato purée
500 g (1 lb) haddock fillet, skinned and cut into large pieces
3 tablespoons lemon juice
175 g (6 oz) courgettes, sliced
salt and pepper to taste
2 tablespoons chopped parsley to garnish

Serves 4
Preparation time:
20 minutes
Cooking time:
30 minutes
Freezing:
Not recommended

1. Heat the oil in a large saucepan, add the onion and fry until softened. Add the green pepper, tomatoes, oregano, potatoes, tomato purée, and salt and pepper. Bring to the boil, then cover and simmer for 20 minutes, until the potatoes are just tender.
2. Meanwhile place the fish, lemon juice, and salt and pepper in a bowl and mix well. Add to the pan with the courgettes, mix gently, cover and cook for 10 minutes, until the fish is tender. Sprinkle with the parsley to serve.

ACE FISH PIE

This is my favourite fish pie. Adding swede to the topping gives it a wonderful golden colour.

750 g ($1\frac{1}{2}$ lb) potatoes, cubed
750 g ($1\frac{1}{2}$ lb) swede, cubed
75 g (3 oz) butter
2 eggs
750 g ($1\frac{1}{2}$ lb) smoked haddock fillet
2 bay leaves
6 peppercorns
450 ml ($\frac{3}{4}$ pint) milk
1 leek, sliced thinly
50 g (2 oz) plain flour
300 ml ($\frac{1}{2}$ pint) white wine
3 tomatoes, skinned and quartered
50 g (2 oz) Cheddar cheese, grated
1 tablespoon sesame seeds
salt and pepper to taste

Serves 6
Preparation time: 1 hour
Cooking time: 20–25 minutes
Freezing: Not recommended

1. Boil the potatoes and swede together for 10–15 minutes, until tender. Drain, add half of the butter, and salt and pepper and mash well. Set aside.
2. Boil the eggs for 7 minutes, shell and cool quickly in cold water. Cut into quarters and set aside.
3. Place the haddock in a pan with the bay leaves, peppercorns and milk. Bring to the boil, then cover and simmer for 12–15 minutes, until tender. Remove the fish, skin and flake into large pieces and set aside. Strain the milk.
4. Melt remaining butter in a pan, add the leek and fry for 5 minutes, until softened. Stir in the flour and cook for 1 minute. Gradually stir in the reserved milk and wine and cook, stirring, until thickened. Remove from the heat and gently stir in the fish, tomatoes, eggs, and salt and pepper.
5. Transfer to a 2.25 litre (4 pint) ovenproof dish and cover with the swede and potato. Fork up the top of the pie and sprinkle with the cheese and sesame seeds. Cook in a preheated oven, 200°C/400°F/Gas Mark 6, for 20–25 minutes, until the top is golden brown. Serve hot.

BAKED FISH WITH RED PEPPER SAUCE

4 cod or haddock fillets, each 175 g (6 oz)
25 g (1 oz) butter, melted
4 tablespoons lemon juice
2 tablespoons oil
2 red peppers, cored, seeded and chopped
1 shallot or small onion, chopped
2 tablespoons double cream
salt and pepper to taste
tarragon sprigs and lemon twists to garnish

1. Place the fish in a shallow buttered baking dish. Brush with the butter, sprinkle with the lemon juice and season with salt and pepper. Cover with foil and cook in a preheated oven, 180°C/350°F/Gas Mark 4, for 20–25 minutes, until tender.
2. Meanwhile, make the sauce. Heat the oil in a small pan, add the red peppers and shallot or onion, cover and cook for about 5 minutes. Add 3 tablespoons water, bring to the boil, cover and cook gently for 15 minutes, until the peppers are tender. Transfer to a blender or food processor and work until smooth. Return to the pan, stir in the cream, and salt and pepper and reheat gently.
3. Transfer the fish to warmed serving plates and surround with the sauce. Garnish with tarragon and lemon.

Serves 4
Preparation time:
20 minutes
Cooking time:
20–25 minutes
Freezing:
Not recommended

CARIBBEAN COD STEW

This is one of those simple recipes I love. A few well chosen ingredients is all you need.

500–750 g (1–1½ lb) cod fillet, skinned and cut into 4 pieces
1 clove garlic, crushed
2 tablespoons olive oil
2 onions, sliced
500 g (1 lb) beefsteak tomatoes, skinned and chopped
2 teaspoons chopped thyme
2 teaspoons soy sauce
salt and pepper to taste

Serves 4
Preparation time: 15 minutes, plus standing time
Cooking time: 22–25 minutes
Freezing: Not recommended

1. Sprinkle the cod with salt and pepper and rub all over with the garlic. Set aside for 15 minutes.
2. Meanwhile, heat the oil in a large saucepan, add the onions and fry gently until softened. Add the tomatoes, thyme and soy sauce, bring to the boil, then partly cover and simmer for 10 minutes, until pulpy.
3. Add the fish, cover and cook for 12–15 minutes, until tender. Serve with steamed or boiled potatoes or yams.

COD WITH BACON LATTICE

This dish is easy to prepare and cook, and looks as good as it tastes. I have chosen cod, but other white fish could be used—try plaice, sole, haddock or whiting.

4 cod fillets, each weighing about 175 g (6 oz)
2 teaspoons finely chopped fresh root ginger
2 rashers back bacon, derinded and cut lengthways into strips
2 spring onions, sliced diagonally
1 tablespoon light soy sauce
salt to taste

Serves 4
Preparation time: 10 minutes, plus standing time
Cooking time: 8–10 minutes
Freezing: Not recommended

1. Sprinkle the cod with salt and ginger and leave to stand for 10 minutes—this will firm the fish. Place on a large heatproof plate and arrange a lattice of bacon strips over each piece. Arrange pieces of spring onion in between the bacon. Sprinkle with the soy sauce.
2. Place in a steamer, on a steaming rack of a wok, or over a large saucepan of simmering water, cover tightly and steam for 8–10 minutes, until the fish is tender and flakes easily.
3. Serve the fish immediately, with boiled rice and a lightly cooked green vegetable.

PARMESAN PLAICE

25 g (1 oz) butter
1 tablespoon oil
4 plaice fillets, each weighing about 175 g (6 oz)
2 tablespoons grated Parmesan cheese
1 tablespoon fresh or dried breadcrumbs
salt and pepper to taste
lemon slices to garnish

1. Put the butter and oil in a grill pan and place under a preheated medium grill until the butter has melted. Add the plaice, skin side down, baste well and sprinkle with salt and pepper.
2. Place under the grill for 3–4 minutes, until half cooked, baste again and top with the cheese and breadcrumbs. Return to the grill for about 3 minutes, until the topping is browned and the fish is cooked. Garnish with lemon.

Serves 4
Preparation time:
10 minutes
Cooking time:
6–7 minutes
Freezing:
Not recommended

HADDOCK AND SPINACH BAKE

500 g (1 lb) spinach
500 g (1 lb) haddock fillet, skinned
2 tablespoons oil
1 onion, chopped
2 celery sticks, chopped
1 green pepper, cored, seeded and chopped
350 g (12 oz) tomatoes, skinned and quartered
1 tablespoon tomato purée
150 ml (1/4 pint) white wine
5 tablespoons vegetable stock
500 g (1 lb) potatoes, cooked, then sliced thinly
salt and pepper to taste

Serves 4
Preparation time:
35 minutes
Cooking time:
30 minutes
Freezing:
Not recommended

1. Place the spinach in a large saucepan with only the water clinging to the leaves after washing. Cover and cook for about 5 minutes, until just wilted. Drain well, then chop and season with salt and pepper. Spread over the base of an oiled 1.75 litre (3 pint) ovenproof dish.
2. Cut the haddock into pieces and place on the spinach.
3. Heat the oil in a large frying pan, add the onion and celery and fry until softened. Add the green pepper and tomatoes and stir well. Add the tomato purée, wine and stock, bring to the boil, then simmer for 5 minutes. Season with salt and pepper.
4. Pour the vegetables over the fish and arrange the potatoes over the top. Cook in a preheated oven, 190°C/375°F/Gas Mark 5, for 30 minutes until the potatoes are golden brown. Serve hot.

HADDOCK IN SPICED YOGURT

The spiced yogurt mixture is similar to tandoori mix, but the spicing is more subtle.

4 haddock fillets, each weighing about 175 g (6 oz), skinned
1 tablespoon chopped fresh root ginger
2 cloves garlic, crushed
1 green chilli, seeded and chopped
1 teaspoon ground cumin
1/2 teaspoon turmeric
1/4 teaspoon chilli powder
1 rounded teaspoon paprika
2 tablespoons lemon juice
150 g (5.3 oz) carton natural yogurt
1 tablespoon oil
1 onion, sliced thinly
salt and pepper to taste
TO SERVE:
shredded lettuce
sliced cucumber
lime wedges

1. Sprinkle the fish with salt and leave for 10 minutes, then pat dry with kitchen paper.
2. Place the ginger, garlic and chilli in a blender or food processor and work until almost smooth. Add the spices, lemon juice, yogurt, and salt and pepper and blend thoroughly.
3. Place the fish in a shallow dish and pour over the marinade, rubbing it in well. Cover and leave for 1–2 hours, if possible.
4. Place a greased rack in a roasting tin one third filled with hot water. Place the fish on the rack and cook in a preheated oven, 200°C/400°F/Gas Mark 6, for 30 minutes, until the fish is tender and the coating darkened in colour.
5. Just before the fish is ready, heat the oil in a frying pan until it is very hot. Add the onion and fry quickly until golden brown.
6. Serve the fish with lettuce and cucumber and sprinkle the fried onion over the top. Garnish with lime and accompany with spiced rice and poppadums.

Serves 4
Preparation time:
30 minutes, plus marinating
Cooking time:
30 minutes
Freezing:
Not recommended

MARINATED FISH KEBABS

750 g (1½ lb) monkfish, halibut or huss, boned, skinned and cut into 2.5 cm (1 inch) cubes
75 g (3 oz) desiccated coconut
1 clove garlic, crushed
2 teaspoons finely chopped fresh root ginger
2 tablespoons finely chopped spring onion
½ teaspoon chilli powder
1 teaspoon ground coriander
½ teaspoon turmeric
1 onion, quartered and separated
1 small red pepper, cored, seeded and cut into 2.5 cm (1 inch) cubes
oil for brushing
salt to taste

Serves 4
Preparation time:
30 minutes, plus marinating
Cooking time:
8–10 minutes
Freezing:
Not recommended

1. Place the fish in a bowl and sprinkle with salt.
2. Place the coconut in a bowl and pour over 150 ml (¼ pint) boiling water. Leave for 15 minutes, then strain, pressing out as much liquid as possible. Add the garlic, ginger, spring onion, chilli powder, coriander and turmeric to the coconut liquid. Mix well, pour over the fish and leave to marinate for at least 1 hour.
3. Thread the fish, onion and red pepper alternately onto 4 skewers. Brush the kebabs with a little oil and cook under a preheated medium grill for 8–10 minutes, turning occasionally, until the fish is tender. Serve immediately, with rice and salad.

TARA PATTIES

750 g ($1\frac{1}{2}$ lb) potatoes
125 g (4 oz) smoked cod's roe
1 onion, grated
1 clove garlic, crushed
1 tablespoon lemon juice
50 g (2 oz) dried wholemeal breadcrumbs
2 tablespoons chopped parsley
1 egg, beaten
2 tablespoons sunflower oil
pepper to taste

1. Boil the potatoes until tender, then mash and leave to cool.
2. Halve the roe and scoop out the inside with a teaspoon, scraping as much as possible from the skin. Place in a bowl with the onion, garlic and lemon juice and mix well with a fork. Add the potatoes and pepper and mix thoroughly. Shape into 8 patties with floured hands.
3. Mix the breadcrumbs and parsley together.
4. Dip the patties in the egg, then in the breadcrumb mixture. Chill for 30 minutes, if possible.
5. Heat the oil in a large frying pan, add the patties in batches and fry for 3–5 minutes, turning once, until golden brown and cooked to your liking. Serve piping hot with Greek salad and pitta bread.

Serves 4
Preparation time: 40 minutes, plus chilling
Cooking time: 3–5 minutes per batch
Freezing: Recommended

GRILLED PLAICE WITH HERB BUTTER SAUCE

Plaice, lemon sole or any fine-flavoured fish is made very special with this subtle butter sauce.

1 small shallot, chopped finely
1 tablespoon tarragon vinegar
2 tablespoons dry white wine
75 g (3 oz) unsalted butter
1 tablespoon chopped herbs, e.g. tarragon, mint, chervil, chives
4 plaice fillets, each weighing about 125 g (4 oz)
oil for brushing
salt and pepper to taste
TO GARNISH:
lemon slices, quartered
chervil sprigs

Serves 4
Preparation time: 15 minutes
Cooking time: 5–6 minutes
Freezing: Not recommended

1. Place the shallot, vinegar and wine in a small pan and simmer gently for about 5 minutes, until reduced to about 1 tablespoon.
2. Remove from the heat and add the butter in tiny pieces, whisking constantly; if the mixture becomes too stiff, return to the heat very briefly. When all the butter has been added you should have a smooth sauce. Stir in the herbs, and salt and pepper. Keep warm.
3. Brush the plaice with a little oil and season with salt and pepper. Cook under a preheated medium grill for 5–6 minutes, until tender.
4. Transfer to 4 individual warmed plates and pour over the sauce. Garnish with lemon and chervil, and serve with mangetouts or peas.

HADDOCK AND BROCCOLI PUFF PIE

Stir-frying the broccoli briefly before adding to the pie ensures it keeps its bright green colour and crisp texture.

250 g (8 oz) broccoli
2 tablespoons oil
500 g (1 lb) haddock fillet, skinned and cubed
125 g (4 oz) button mushrooms, sliced
62.5 g (2.2 oz) packet soft cheese with garlic and herbs
142 ml (5 fl oz) carton single cream
1 tablespoon cornflour, blended with 1 tablespoon water
200 g (7 oz) ready-made puff pastry
salt and pepper to taste
beaten egg or milk to glaze

1. Cut the broccoli into small florets, then slice the stalks thinly.
2. Heat half of the oil in a pan, add the broccoli and stir-fry for 1 minute. Add 3 tablespoons water, bring to the boil, then cover and cook for 4 minutes. Transfer to a 1.75 litre (3 pint) pie dish, add the haddock and stir well.
3. Heat the remaining oil in the pan, add the mushrooms and fry briefly until just softened. Gently stir in the cheese until it is softened, add the cream and heat gently. Add the blended cornflour and cook, stirring, until thickened. Season with salt and pepper, then pour into the pie dish, stirring into the fish and broccoli.
4. Roll out the pastry on a floured surface and use to cover the pie. Brush with beaten egg or milk and bake in a preheated oven, 200°C/400°F/Gas Mark 6, for 30–35 minutes, until the pastry is golden. Serve piping hot.

Serves 4
Preparation time:
30 minutes
Cooking time:
30–35 minutes
Freezing:
Not recommended

FISH WITH STIR-FRIED VEGETABLES

Any firm-fleshed fish can be used for this dish, e.g. huss or monkfish. Try it also with a mixture of prawns and white fish. Huss is easy to bone as it has one main bone with smaller bones firmly attached to it.

500 g (1 lb) huss, boned
1 tablespoon cornflour
3 tablespoons oil
2 rashers streaky bacon, derinded and cut into strips
1 leek, shredded
175 g (6 oz) green cabbage, shredded
1 tablespoon light soy sauce
4 tablespoons dry white wine
2 teaspoons chilli sauce
½ teaspoon sugar
75 g (3 oz) beansprouts
salt to taste

Serves 4
Preparation time: 35 minutes, plus standing time
Cooking time: 10–15 minutes
Freezing: Not recommended

1. Cut the fish into thin strips, place in a bowl and sprinkle liberally with salt. Leave for 20 minutes. Pat dry on kitchen paper and toss in the cornflour.
2. Heat the oil in a large frying pan or wok, add the fish and stir-fry for 3–4 minutes, until it feels firm. Remove with a slotted spoon and drain on kitchen paper.
3. Add the bacon to the pan and stir-fry over a high heat until it starts to crisp. Add the leek and cabbage and stir-fry for 2–3 minutes, until the cabbage has started to wilt.
4. Mix together the soy sauce, wine, chilli sauce, sugar and 3 tablespoons water. Add to the pan with the fish and stir well. Lower the heat, cover and cook for 2–3 minutes. Add the beansprouts and cook for 1 minute. Serve immediately, with boiled rice or Chinese noodles.

STIR-FRIED SCALLOPS WITH 'SEAWEED'

Seaweed on the menu in Chinese restaurants is often spring greens in disguise. They go wonderfully well with scallops, or any other seafood for that matter.

1 tablespoon blanched almonds
500 g (1 lb) spring greens or dark cabbage, tough stalks removed
15 g (½ oz) butter
1 tablespoon oil
1 shallot or small onion, cut into rings
500 g (1 lb) queen or small scallops
1 teaspoon caster sugar
2 tablespoons dry sherry
salt and pepper to taste
oil for deep-frying

1. Cut the almonds lengthways into shreds. Place under a preheated medium grill until browned. Set aside.
2. Shred the greens or cabbage very finely.
3. Melt the butter and oil in a pan, add the shallot or onion and scallops and cook for 3–4 minutes, stirring gently. Season with salt and pepper, remove the scallops and onion from the pan and keep warm. Set the pan aside.
4. Carefully add the greens or cabbage to the hot oil in batches, count to ten, then quickly remove and drain on kitchen paper. Mix in the sugar and salt and keep warm.
5. Add the sherry to the scallop pan and boil to reduce and thicken. Season with salt and pepper.
6. Arrange the greens or cabbage on 4 individual warmed serving plates. Place the scallops in the centre, pour over the sauce and sprinkle with the almonds to serve.

Serves 4
Preparation time:
25 minutes
Cooking time:
10 minutes
Freezing:
Not recommended

SPICED RICE WITH PRAWNS

3 tablespoons oil
1 onion, chopped
1 clove garlic, crushed
1 teaspoon ground coriander
½ teaspoon chilli powder
1 teaspoon ground cumin
1 teaspoon curry powder
250 g (8 oz) peeled prawns (thawed if frozen)
1 tablespoon soy sauce
125 g (4 oz) frozen peas
250 g (8 oz) long-grain rice, cooked
1 egg, beaten
1 tablespoon chopped spring onion
salt and pepper to taste

Serves 4
Preparation time: 20 minutes
Cooking time: About 15 minutes
Freezing: Not recommended

1. Heat 2 tablespoons of the oil in a large pan, add the onion and fry until softened. Add the garlic, coriander, chilli powder, cumin and curry powder, stir well and cook for 1 minute.
2. Stir in the prawns until they are well coated, then add the soy sauce, peas, 4 tablespoons water, and salt and pepper. Cook for 2 minutes.
3. Add the rice, mix thoroughly, then cover and cook gently until thoroughly heated through.
4. Meanwhile, make the omelette. Beat together the egg, 2 tablespoons water, and salt and pepper. Heat the remaining oil in a frying pan, add the egg and cook until just set. Slide onto a plate, roll up and cut into strips.
5. Turn the rice mixture onto a warmed serving dish and arrange the egg strips on top. Sprinkle with the spring onion and serve immediately.

RED MULLET IN VINE LEAVES

This stunning dish has an excellent flavour to match. Try it with trout too.

4 red mullet, each weighing about 250 g (8 oz), gutted and scaled
2 tablespoons olive oil
2 tablespoons lemon juice
1 teaspoon coriander seeds, cracked
1 tablespoon chopped thyme
1 clove garlic, crushed
10–12 large vine leaves
salt and pepper to taste
lemon wedges to garnish

1. Place the mullet in a large shallow dish. Mix together the oil, lemon juice, coriander seeds, thyme, garlic, and salt and pepper. Pour over the fish, making sure it goes

inside the cavity. Leave for about 1 hour in a cool place.
2. If the vine leaves are in brine, rinse them thoroughly, cover with boiling water and leave for 20 minutes; drain and dry.
3. Wrap the fish in the vine leaves, tucking the ends underneath. Place in an oiled baking dish and cook in a preheated oven, 180°C/350°F/Gas Mark 4, for 25–30 minutes. Alternatively, cook on a barbecue for 15–20 minutes, turning once. Garnish with lemon wedges to serve.

Serves 4
Preparation time:
20 minutes, plus marinating
Cooking time:
25–30 minutes or 15–20 minutes on a barbecue
Freezing:
Not recommended

CIDERED FISH CRUMBLE

Huss is a rather under-rated fish. Its soft delicate flesh stays moist and does not break up during cooking. Any firm-fleshed fish could be used instead.

25 g (1 oz) butter or margarine
1 onion, chopped
25 g (1 oz) plain flour
300 ml (½ pint) dry cider
300 ml (½ pint) vegetable stock
2 carrots, grated
250 g (8 oz) celeriac, grated
500 g (1 lb) huss, boned and cubed
1 tablespoon lemon juice
1 tablespoon chopped parsley
25 g (1 oz) wholemeal breadcrumbs
50 g (2 oz) Cheddar cheese, grated
1 tablespoon sesame seeds
salt and pepper to taste

Serves 4
Preparation time: 20 minutes
Cooking time: 40 minutes
Freezing: Recommended

1. Melt the butter or margarine in a large saucepan, add the onion and fry until softened. Stir in the flour and cook for 1 minute. Gradually stir in the cider and stock and cook, stirring, until thickened and smooth.
2. Add the carrots, celeriac, huss, lemon juice, parsley, and salt and pepper. Mix well, then transfer to a 1.75 litre (3 pint) ovenproof dish.
3. Mix together the breadcrumbs, cheese and sesame seeds and sprinkle over the top. Cook in a preheated oven, 180°C/350°F/Gas Mark 4, for 40 minutes, until the topping is crisp and golden brown. Serve with broccoli or peas.

PERFECT FRIED FISH

Try this extra light batter and fish and chips will never be the same again! Use fresh, not frozen, fish for the best flavour.

4 cod or haddock fillets, each weighing 175 g (6 oz)
seasoned plain flour for coating
175 g (6 oz) self-raising flour
½ teaspoon salt
250 ml (8 fl oz) water or beer
pepper to taste
oil for deep-frying

1. Dust the fish with seasoned flour.
2. Sift the self-raising flour, salt and plenty of pepper into a

mixing bowl. Gradually stir in the water or beer, beating well to form a smooth batter.

3. Heat the oil in a large pan to 180°C/350°F or until a little batter dropped into it rises instantly to the surface and starts to brown. Dip the fish, one piece at a time, into the batter, shaking off as much excess as possible. Deep-fry 2 pieces at a time for 6–8 minutes, depending on the thickness of the fillet. Drain well on kitchen paper.

4. Serve with chips, and lemon wedges and salad if you wish.

Serves 4
Preparation time:
15 minutes
Cooking time:
6–8 minutes per batch
Freezing:
Not recommended

BAKED FISH PASTA

Pesto—the Italian basil-flavoured sauce—is available ready-made in jars.

1 tablespoon oil
1 onion, chopped
1 carrot, chopped
1 celery stick, chopped
397 g (14 oz) can tomatoes
150 ml (1/4 pint) vegetable or fish stock
1 tablespoon pesto
175 g (6 oz) pasta shapes
500 g (1 lb) cod fillet, skinned and cubed
175 g (6 oz) Mozzarella cheese, sliced thinly
salt and pepper to taste

Serves 4
Preparation time: 35 minutes
Cooking time: 25 minutes
Freezing: Not recommended

1. Heat the oil in a saucepan, add the onion and fry until softened. Add the carrot and celery and cook for 5 minutes. Add the tomatoes with their juice, stock, and salt and pepper and bring to the boil. Simmer, uncovered, for 10–15 minutes, until thickened, then stir in the pesto. Remove from heat.
2. Meanwhile, cook the pasta according to packet instructions, drain and place in an oiled 1.75 litre (3 pint) ovenproof dish.
3. Add the fish to the pasta and mix well. Pour over the sauce and mix lightly. Arrange the Mozzarella over the top. Cook in a preheated oven, 190°C/375°F/Gas Mark 5, for 25 minutes, until the cheese topping has melted. Serve with a green salad.

LEMON SOLE WITH TARRAGON AND GRAPES

4–6 lemon sole fillets, depending on size, skinned
5 tablespoons dry white wine
few peppercorns
1 shallot, sliced thinly
1 bay leaf
few tarragon sprigs
2 slices lemon
1 teaspoon chopped tarragon
4 tablespoons double cream
125 g (4 oz) seedless white grapes
salt and pepper to taste
tarragon sprigs to garnish

1. Cut each fillet lengthways into 6 strips. Place in a frying pan and add the wine, peppercorns, shallot, bay leaf, tarragon sprigs and lemon. Bring to simmering point and cook for about 5 minutes, until tender. Transfer carefully

with a fish slice to a warmed serving plate and keep warm.
2. Strain the pan juices, then return to the pan and cook over high heat until reduced by half. Lower the heat, stir in the chopped tarragon, cream and grapes and heat through gently. Season with salt and pepper. Pour over the fish.
3. Garnish with tarragon and serve with courgettes or mangetouts and steamed potatoes.

Serves 4
Preparation time:
15 minutes
Cooking time:
10 minutes
Freezing:
Not recommended

DANISH HERRING SALAD

6 pickled herring fillets
1 red onion
1 red dessert apple
142 ml (5 fl oz) carton soured cream
3 spring onions, chopped
1 tablespoon snipped chives
salt and pepper to taste
shredded lettuce to serve

Serves 4
Preparation time: 20 minutes
Freezing: Not recommended

1. Slice the herrings diagonally into strips. Cut the onion into quarters, then slice as thinly as possible. Quarter, core, and slice the apple. Mix the herring, onion and apple together and set aside.
2. Mix together the soured cream, spring onions, half of the chives, and salt and pepper.
3. Arrange the lettuce on 4 individual plates. Top with the salad and dressing and sprinkle with remaining chives.

SEAFOOD PASTA SALAD

250 g (8 oz) tricolore pasta
500 g (1 lb) cod fillet
3 teaspoons soy sauce
4 spring onions, cut into matchstick pieces
125 g (4 oz) button mushrooms, sliced
125 g (4 oz) courgettes, sliced thinly
50 g (2 oz) peeled prawns (thawed if frozen)
2 tablespoons white wine vinegar
3 tablespoons sunflower oil
1 teaspoon finely grated fresh root ginger
salt and pepper to taste

Serves 4–6
Preparation time: 20 minutes
Cooking time: 10–12 minutes
Freezing: Not recommended

1. Cook the pasta in boiling salted water according to packet instructions, then drain, rinse under running cold water and set aside.
2. Place the fish on a heatproof plate and sprinkle with 1 teaspoon of the soy sauce. Steam in a wok with a steaming rack or tightly covered over a large saucepan of boiling water for 10–12 minutes. Remove and, when cool enough to handle, skin and cut into chunks.
3. Mix together the pasta, spring onions, mushrooms, courgettes and prawns. Carefully stir in the cod.
4. Shake the remaining soy sauce in a screw-top jar with the vinegar, oil, ginger, and salt and pepper. Pour over the salad, mix gently, cover and chill until required.

SMOKED TROUT PARCELS

1 smoked trout, weighing 350 g (12 oz)
250 g (8 oz) spinach
25 g (1 oz) butter or margarine
1 small leek, shredded
50 g (2 oz) button mushrooms, sliced
½ teaspoon chopped oregano
1 tablespoon lemon juice
25 g (1 oz) long-grain rice, cooked
3 tablespoons soured cream
250 g (8 oz) ready-made puff pastry
beaten egg to glaze
salt and pepper to taste
TO SERVE:
few lettuce leaves
soured cream

Serves 4
Preparation time: 35 minutes
Cooking time: 20 minutes
Freezing: Recommended

1. Skin the trout and remove the bones. Flake the fish into a bowl.
2. Place the spinach in a saucepan with just the water clinging to the leaves after washing, cover and cook for 5 minutes, until tender. Drain well, pressing out as much liquid as possible. Chop finely and add to the fish.
3. Melt the butter or margarine in a small pan, add the leek and fry gently until softened. Add the mushrooms and oregano and cook for 2 minutes. Add to the fish with the lemon juice, rice, cream, and salt and pepper; mix well.
4. Roll out the pastry on a floured surface to a 30 cm (12 inch) square. Cut into four 15 cm (6 inch) squares. Pile the filling along the middle of each square to within 1 cm (½ inch) of the ends. Brush the edges with beaten egg.
5. Slash the pastry diagonally either side of the filling at 1 cm (½ inch) intervals. Fold up the ends, then plait the pastry strips over the filling. Brush with egg.
6. Place the parcels on a dampened baking sheet and bake in a preheated oven, 220°C/425°F/Gas Mark 7, for 20 minutes, until golden brown.
7. Serve each parcel warm, garnished with lettuce leaves and soured cream.

WHITING AND SCALLOP PARCELS

4 whiting fillets, each weighing 175 g (6 oz), skinned
4 small scallops
½ teaspoon chopped thyme
2 spring onions, chopped
1 tablespoon chopped fennel
2 tomatoes, skinned and chopped
4 tablespoons dry vermouth
salt and pepper to taste

1. Starting at the wide end of each whiting, wrap each fillet around a scallop and secure with a wooden cocktail stick. Sprinkle with salt and pepper. Place each roll on a square of foil large enough to enclose it.
2. Mix together the thyme, spring onions and fennel and sprinkle over the fish. Place a little chopped tomato around the fish and sprinkle with the vermouth, and salt and pepper. Fold the foil to enclose the fish in a 'parcel' and place in a baking dish.
3. Cook in a preheated oven, 190°C/375°F/Gas Mark 5, for 20 minutes, until tender. Place a parcel on each individual plate for the diners to open. Serve with soft bread to mop up the juices.

Serves 4
Preparation time:
20 minutes
Cooking time:
20 minutes
Freezing:
Not recommended

SCALLOPS WITH BLACK BEAN SAUCE

Black beans are available in cans or packets—if using packeted beans soak first. With garlic and ginger they give an unforgettable flavour to this dish. Serve it with broccoli and rice for a main meal, or on its own as a starter.

2 tablespoons oil
1 teaspoon finely chopped fresh root ginger
1 clove garlic, crushed
1 tablespoon finely chopped spring onions
1 rounded tablespoon black beans, chopped roughly
500 g (1 lb) scallops
1 tablespoon light soy sauce
1 tablespoon dry sherry

Serves 4
Preparation time: 20 minutes
Cooking time: 4–5 minutes
Freezing: Not recommended

1. Heat the oil in a large frying pan or wok, add the ginger, garlic, spring onions and black beans and stir-fry for 1 minute. Add the scallops and stir-fry for 30 seconds.
2. Add the soy sauce, sherry and 5 tablespoons water. Bring to the boil, then simmer for 4–5 minutes, until the scallops are just cooked.
3. Serve immediately.

TROUT WITH GREEN SAUCE

4 trout, each weighing 250 g (8 oz), gutted
3 tablespoons lime or lemon juice
1 teaspoon dried oregano
2 teaspoons chopped mint
6 tablespoons olive oil
2 cloves garlic, crushed
4 tablespoons chopped parsley
2 teaspoons chopped capers
1 tablespoon lemon juice
salt and pepper to taste

1. Using a sharp knife, make diagonal cuts over both sides of the fish. Place in a dish.
2. Mix together the lime or lemon juice, oregano, mint, half of the oil, and salt and pepper. Pour over the fish, making sure it goes inside the cavity. Leave to marinate for 30 minutes.
3. Meanwhile, mix together the garlic, parsley, capers, lemon juice, and salt and pepper. Gradually beat in the remaining oil until you have a thick sauce.
4. Place the trout in the grill pan and pour over any remaining marinade. Cook under a preheated moderate grill for 10–12 minutes, turning once, until the fish is cooked. Serve immediately, with the green sauce.

Serves 4
Preparation time:
20 minutes, plus marinating
Cooking time:
10–12 minutes
Freezing:
Not recommended

HADDOCK AND TOMATO SOUFFLÉ

50 g (2 oz) butter
1 onion, chopped
50 g (2 oz) plain flour
300 ml (½ pint) milk
250 g (8 oz) smoked haddock fillet, skinned and cubed
2 ripe tomatoes, skinned and quartered
4 eggs, separated
25 g (1 oz) Parmesan cheese, grated finely
salt and pepper to taste

Serves 4
Preparation time: 30 minutes
Cooking time: 35 minutes
Freezing: Not recommended

1. Melt the butter in a saucepan, add the onion and fry gently until softened. Add the flour and cook for 1 minute, stirring. Gradually add the milk, stirring until thickened and smooth. Add the haddock and cook very gently for 5 minutes.
2. Remove from the heat and stir in the tomatoes, egg yolks, and salt and pepper. Set aside 2 tablespoons of the cheese; add the remainder to the sauce.
3. Whisk the egg whites until stiff, then fold into the sauce. Turn into a greased 1.2 litre (2 pint) soufflé dish.
4. Sprinkle with the reserved cheese and bake in a preheated oven, 190°C/375°F/Gas Mark 5, for 35 minutes, until well risen and golden. Serve immediately.

MUSSELS IN WHITE WINE

A plate of steaming mussels served with a crusty French loaf is sheer heaven to me. Use a mussel shell as a spoon to eat them and provide lots of napkins.

1 tablespoon olive oil
2 shallots, chopped
2 cloves garlic, chopped
few parsley stalks
150 ml (¼ pint) dry white wine
2.25 litres (4 pints) fresh mussels, cleaned (see page 8)
1 tablespoon chopped parsley
pepper to taste

Serves 4
Preparation time: 10 minutes
Cooking time: 8–10 minutes
Freezing: Not recommended

1. Heat the oil in a large pan, add the shallots and garlic and fry for 2–3 minutes. Add the parsley stalks and wine, mix well and bring to the boil.
2. Add the mussels, cover and cook for about 5 minutes, shaking the pan occasionally, until the shells open; discard any that do not.
3. Turn into a large serving bowl or 4 individual bowls, sprinkle with the chopped parsley and black pepper and serve immediately.

LEMON SOLE FILLETS WITH PRAWN AND CHERVIL SAUCE

For a special occasion, use Dover sole fillets instead of lemon sole. This dish could also be served on its own as a starter. Purée the sauce if you prefer it smooth.

2 lemon sole, each weighing about 500 g (1 lb), filleted and skinned
25 g (1 oz) butter
1 tablespoon chopped parsley
150 ml (¼ pint) dry white wine
150 ml (¼ pint) fish stock
2 tablespoons double cream
125 g (4 oz) peeled prawns (thawed if frozen), chopped
2 tablespoons chopped chervil
salt and pepper to taste

Serves 4
Preparation time: 30 minutes
Cooking time: 8–10 minutes
Freezing: Not recommended

1. Make a few small cuts down the skinned side of the fillets to stop them curling up. Sprinkle with salt, pepper and parsley. Place a knob of butter on top.
2. Fold the fillets in half and place in a large frying pan. Pour over the wine and stock and bring to a simmer. Cover with buttered greaseproof paper and cook for 8–10 minutes, until cooked. Transfer carefully with a fish slice to 4 individual warmed plates and keep warm.
3. Boil the pan juices until reduced by half. Lower the heat and stir in the cream, prawns, chervil and seasoning. Pour around the fish and serve with new potatoes and salad.

FISH QUENELLES WITH SPINACH AND MUSHROOMS

Quenelles are velvety dumplings of minced fish lightened with egg white and cream. The mixture can be made the day before it is cooked, as it is best well chilled.

250 g (8 oz) whiting or hake fillets, skinned and chopped
2 small egg whites (size 5), lightly beaten
pinch of cayenne pepper
142 ml (5 fl oz) carton single cream
500 g (1 lb) spinach leaves or 250 g (8 oz) frozen leaf spinach, thawed
50 g (2 oz) butter
125 g (4 oz) button mushrooms
1 tablespoon lemon juice
1 tablespoon grated Parmesan cheese
salt and pepper to taste

1. Place the fish in a food processor and work until smooth. Add the egg whites, cayenne, and salt and pepper and mix well. Gradually blend in the cream, then transfer to a bowl and chill until firm.
2. If using fresh spinach, place in a pan with just the water clinging to the leaves after washing, cover and cook for about 5 minutes, until tender. Drain well, pressing out the excess water.
3. Form the fish mixture into egg shapes using 2 tablespoons, then place carefully in a lightly buttered shallow pan, in one layer. Cover with boiling water, cover the pan and cook gently for about 10 minutes.
4. Meanwhile, heat half of the butter in a saucepan, add the mushrooms and fry for about 3 minutes, until softened. Stir in the spinach and heat through. Transfer to a warmed serving dish and keep warm.
5. Melt the remaining butter in a small pan and add the lemon juice and pepper. Remove the quenelles with a slotted spoon and arrange on the spinach. Pour over the butter and sprinkle with the Parmesan. Serve immediately.

Serves 4
Preparation time:
40 minutes, plus chilling
Cooking time:
10 minutes
Freezing:
Not recommended

GRILLED PLAICE WITH CRISPY BACON

4 plaice fillets, each weighing about 175 g (6 oz)
2 tablespoons lemon juice
125 g (4 oz) smoked streaky bacon, derinded and chopped
1 tablespoon small parsley sprigs
salt and pepper to taste
oil for brushing
lemon wedges to serve

Serves 4
Preparation time: 15 minutes
Cooking time: 4–5 minutes
Freezing: Not recommended

1. Place the fish on an oiled grill rack, sprinkle with salt and pepper, brush with a little oil and sprinkle with half of the lemon juice. Grill on one side only for 4–5 minutes, until tender.
2. Meanwhile, place the bacon in a cold pan and heat gently until the fat runs. Increase the heat and fry until the bacon is crispy. Add the parsley and fry for 1 minute, then stir in the remaining lemon juice and pepper.
3. Transfer the fish to 4 warmed plates, sprinkle with the bacon and parsley, and garnish with lemon wedges.

SPICED MACKEREL WITH YOGURT SAUCE

2 mackerel, each weighing about 500 g (1 lb), gutted and heads removed
½ teaspoon chilli powder
2 teaspoons curry powder
1 teaspoon ground coriander
1 teaspoon turmeric
1 teaspoon garam masala
150 g (5.3 oz) carton natural yogurt
5 cm (2 inch) piece cucumber, chopped finely
salt to taste
oil for frying
mint sprigs to garnish

Serves 4
Preparation time: 15 minutes, plus standing time
Cooking time: About 4 minutes per batch
Freezing: Not recommended

1. Cut the fish crossways into steaks about 3.5 cm (1½ inches) thick—you will need a sharp knife for this.
2. Mix together the spices and salt on a plate, then toss in the fish, rubbing in well. Leave to stand for 15 minutes.
3. Mix together the yogurt, cucumber and a little salt.
4. Heat about a 2.5 cm (1 inch) depth of oil in a large pan. Add the fish, in batches if necessary, and fry on all sides for about 4 minutes, until golden and tender. Drain well on kitchen paper.
5. Transfer to warmed serving plates and garnish with mint sprigs. Serve with the yogurt sauce, spiced rice and poppadums, if you wish.

GRILLED TROUT WITH PESTO AND TOMATO SAUCE

Pesto, available ready-made in jars, marries particularly well with tomatoes in this trout dish.

2 tablespoons olive oil
4 ripe tomatoes, skinned and chopped
3 anchovy fillets, chopped finely (optional)
4 trout, each weighing about 250 g (8 oz), gutted
2 tablespoons pesto
salt and pepper to taste
parsley sprigs to garnish

Serves 4
Preparation time: 20 minutes
Cooking time: 10–12 minutes
Freezing: Not recommended

1. Heat the oil in a frying pan, add the tomatoes and fry gently for about 5 minutes. Season with pepper and add the anchovies, if using. Keep warm.
2. Season the trout inside and out with salt and pepper. Cook under a preheated medium grill for 5–6 minutes on each side.
3. Just before serving, stir the pesto into the tomato sauce. Pour a little sauce over each fish and garnish with parsley sprigs to serve.

EGG FU-YUNG

Rustle up this stylish snack in a few minutes—perfect for late-night feasts.

12 raw Mediterranean prawns, peeled
6 eggs
1 tablespoon dry sherry
1 tablespoon light soy sauce
pinch of sugar
2 tablespoons oil
salt and pepper to taste
3 spring onions, chopped finely, to garnish

Serves 4
Preparation time: 15 minutes
Cooking time: 5–6 minutes
Freezing: Not recommended

1. Cut the prawns down the back and remove the black intestine. Rinse and dry well.
2. Beat together the eggs, sherry, soy sauce, 4 tablespoons water, sugar, and salt and pepper.
3. Heat the oil in a large pan or wok, add the prawns and stir-fry for 2–3 minutes, until they turn pink. Remove with a slotted spoon.
4. Add the egg mixture and stir-fry until it starts to set. Return the prawns to the pan and cook for 1 minute.
5. Sprinkle with the spring onions to serve.

JACKET POTATOES WITH POTTED SHRIMPS

Keep some potted shrimps in the freezer for this excellent standby snack.

2 tablespoons oil
1 teaspoon paprika
1 teaspoon coarse grain mustard
4 large potatoes, washed
2 × 100 g (3½ oz) pots frozen potted shrimps, thawed
2 teaspoons chopped dill or parsley
sea salt and pepper to taste
dill or parsley sprigs to garnish

Serves 4
Preparation time: 10 minutes
Cooking time: 1–1¼ hours
Freezing: Not recommended

1. Mix together the oil, paprika, mustard, and sea salt and pepper on a plate. Roll the potatoes in this mixture until well coated. Place on a baking sheet and cook in a preheated oven, 200°C/400°F/Gas Mark 6, for 1–1¼ hours, until cooked.
2. Cut a cross in the top of each potato and squeeze them to open out the cut edges. Place a spoonful of potted shrimps on top and sprinkle with the chopped herbs. Serve immediately, garnished with dill or parsley.

HADDOCK STUFFED POTATOES

4 large potatoes, washed
1 tablespoon oil
1 tablespoon chopped mixed herbs, e.g. rosemary, sage, thyme
250 g (8 oz) smoked haddock fillet
3 spring onions, chopped
75 g (3 oz) cooked sweetcorn kernels
4 tablespoons milk
75 g (3 oz) Cheddar cheese, grated
salt and pepper to taste
watercress sprigs to garnish

Serves 4
Preparation time: 25 minutes
Cooking time: 1¼–1½ hours
Freezing: Recommended

1. Brush the potatoes with the oil, then sprinkle with the herbs, and salt and pepper. Place on a baking sheet and bake in a preheated oven, 200°C/400°F/Gas Mark 6, for 1–1¼ hours, until tender.
2. Place the haddock in a frying pan with water to cover. Bring to the boil, then cover and simmer for 10–12 minutes, until the fish flakes easily. Remove from the pan with a fish slice, then skin and flake the fish.
3. Cut the potatoes in half and scoop out the insides into a bowl. Mash well, then mix in the spring onions, sweetcorn,

milk, half of the cheese, and salt and pepper. Mix well, then gently fold in the fish.
4. Pile the filling back into the potato shells and sprinkle with remaining cheese. Return to the oven for 15 minutes, until golden. Serve hot, garnished with watercress.

HADDOCK AND WATERCRESS TART

FOR THE PASTRY:
75 g (3 oz) self-raising wholemeal flour
75 g (3 oz) plain flour, sifted
75 g (3 oz) margarine
2 tablespoons cold water
FOR THE FILLING:
350 g (12 oz) smoked haddock fillet
300 ml (½ pint) milk
40 g (1½ oz) butter
1 shallot or small onion, chopped finely
1 celery stick, chopped
25 g (1 oz) plain flour
½ bunch watercress, chopped finely
2 eggs, beaten
1 tablespoon grated Parmesan cheese
salt and pepper to taste

Serves 4–6
Preparation time:
45 minutes, plus chilling
Cooking time:
25–30 minutes
Freezing:
Recommended

1. To make the shortcrust pastry, mix the flours together in a bowl, then rub in the fat until the mixture resembles breadcrumbs. Add the water and mix to a firm dough. Turn onto a lightly floured surface and knead briefly, then roll out and use to line a 20–23 cm (8–9 inch) deep flan tin. Chill for 15 minutes.
2. Line the pastry case with foil, fill with baking beans and bake blind in a preheated oven, 200°C/400°F/Gas Mark 6, for 15 minutes. Remove the beans and foil. Lower the temperature to 190°C/375°F/Gas Mark 5.
3. Meanwhile, place the haddock and milk in a pan and bring to the boil. Lower the heat, cover and cook for 8–10 minutes, until the fish flakes easily. Remove with a fish slice, skin and flake the fish and set aside; reserve the milk.
4. Heat the butter in a pan, add the shallot or onion and celery and cook until softened. Stir in the flour and cook for 1 minute. Gradually stir in the reserved milk and cook, stirring, until thickened. Remove from the heat. Stir in the fish, watercress, eggs, and salt and pepper.
5. Pour into the flan case, sprinkle with the Parmesan and return to the oven for 25–30 minutes, until the filling is risen and golden brown. Serve warm or cold.

MUSSEL AND LEEK TARTS

1 quantity shortcrust pastry (see above)
600 ml (1 pint) fresh mussels, cleaned (see page 8)
4 tablespoons dry white wine
25 g (1 oz) butter
2 leeks, sliced
pinch of turmeric
3 tablespoons natural fromage frais
salt and pepper to taste
pinch of paprika

1. Divide the pastry into 4 and roll out each piece to line a 10 cm (4 inch) tart tin. Line with foil and beans and bake blind in a preheated oven, 200°C/400°F/Gas Mark 6, for 15 minutes. Remove the paper and beans and return to the oven for 10 minutes.
2. Meanwhile, make the filling. Place the mussels and wine in a large pan, cover and cook over high heat for about 5 minutes, until the shells open; discard any that do not. Drain, reserving the liquid, remove the mussels from their shells and set aside.
3. Heat the butter in a saucepan, add the leeks and cook until softened. Strain the reserved cooking liquor into the pan, add the turmeric and simmer for 5 minutes. Add the mussels and heat through.
4. Lower the heat, stir in the fromage frais and heat through without boiling. Taste and add pepper, and a little salt if necessary.
5. Fill the warm pastry cases with the mussel mixture. Sprinkle with paprika and serve warm.

Serves 4
Preparation time:
30 minutes
Cooking time:
25 minutes
Freezing:
Not recommended

IRISH BAKED SALMON

1 salmon, weighing 1 kg (2 lb), gutted and scaled
50 g (2 oz) unsalted butter
handful of parsley sprigs
150 ml (¼ pint) dry white wine
2 tablespoons lemon juice
142 ml (5 fl oz) carton double cream
salt and pepper to taste
parsley sprigs and lemon to garnish

Serves 6
Preparation time:
20 minutes
Cooking time:
30–40 minutes
Freezing:
Not recommended

1. Place the salmon in a baking dish and sprinkle inside and out with salt and pepper. Dot the inside with a little butter and stuff with the parsley. Dot the remaining butter over the top. Pour over the wine and cover with foil.
2. Cook in a preheated oven, 180°C/350°F/Gas Mark 4, for 30–40 minutes, until tender. Carefully transfer the salmon to a warmed serving dish with a fish slice and keep warm.
3. Strain the liquor into a small pan and boil until reduced by one third. Add the lemon juice, then lower the heat and gently stir in the cream. Heat through gently.
4. Garnish the fish with parsley and lemon. Serve with the sauce, new potatoes and a green vegetable.

CHINESE STEAMED BASS

750 g (1½ lb) sea bass, gutted and scaled
sea salt
2.5 cm (1 inch) piece fresh root ginger
6 spring onions
1 tablespoon light soy sauce
1 tablespoon oil
1 clove garlic, sliced thinly

Serves 4–6
Preparation time:
25 minutes, plus standing time
Cooking time:
About 15 minutes
Freezing:
Not recommended

1. Sprinkle the fish with sea salt. Leave for 15 minutes.
2. Peel the ginger and cut into fine matchstick pieces.
3. Cut the spring onions into long shreds.
4. Place the fish on a heatproof plate and sprinkle with the ginger, spring onions and soy sauce. Place on a steaming rack inside a wok containing a 2.5 cm (1 inch) depth of boiling water. (Alternatively place the plate over a large pan of boiling water.) Cover with a tightly fitting lid or foil and steam for about 15 minutes, until just tender.
5. Just before serving, heat the oil in a pan, add the garlic and fry until golden brown. Quickly pour over the fish and serve immediately, with rice and stir-fried vegetables.

PRAWN AND SCALLOP CRACKERS WITH PINK PEPPERCORN SAUCE

Fillo pastry is wafer thin and very crisp and light when cooked. Keep it covered with clingfilm until ready to use to avoid it becoming brittle. You can substitute green peppercorns for the pink ones if you wish.

350 g (12 oz) cooked prawns in shell
2 tablespoons lemon juice
6 tablespoons dry white wine
1 teaspoon pink peppercorns
8 scallops
1 tablespoon chopped parsley
2 tablespoons snipped chives
1 tablespoon chopped mint
pinch of chilli powder
75 g (3 oz) unsalted butter
125 g (4 oz) fillo pastry (4 sheets)
salt and pepper to taste
few chives to finish

Serves 4
Preparation time: 25 minutes
Cooking time: 12–15 minutes
Freezing: Not recommended

1. Set aside 8 prawns for garnish; shell the remainder.
2. Place the lemon juice, wine and peppercorns in a large pan and bring to the boil. Add the scallops, cover and simmer for 2–3 minutes, until they start to become firm and white. Remove with a slotted spoon, cut each into 3 pieces and place in a bowl with the peeled prawns, herbs, chilli powder, and salt and pepper. Mix well. Reserve the cooking liquid.
3. Melt 25 g (1 oz) of the butter. Cut a sheet of fillo into 4 squares and stack on top of each other, brushing each piece with butter. Arrange a quarter of the fish mixture along the centre of the pastry stack, roll up, gather at each end like a cracker and tie with fine string. Repeat to make 4 crackers.
4. Place on a greased baking sheet, brush with butter and bake in a preheated oven, 190°C/375°F/Gas Mark 5, for 12–15 minutes, until crisp and golden.
5. Boil the reserved liquid until it is reduced to about 1 tablespoon. Remove from the heat and beat in the remaining butter a small piece at a time, until a shiny sauce is formed; return to the heat briefly if the sauce becomes too thick. Taste and add a little salt if necessary.
6. Place the crackers on 4 individual warmed plates and carefully remove the string. Replace it with strands of chive tied in a knot. Pour a little sauce around the crackers and garnish with the reserved prawns. Serve with a green vegetable, such as mangetouts.

CARTERET SKATE

Carteret is a seaside resort in Normandy where I first tried this deliciously piquant dish.

2 shallots or small onions, chopped
2 bay leaves
1 clove
few celery leaves
6 tablespoons cider vinegar
4 skate wings
142 ml (5 fl oz) carton double cream
2 teaspoons chopped capers
2 tablespoons chopped parsley
salt and pepper to taste
parsley sprigs to garnish

1. Place the shallots or onions, bay leaves, clove, celery leaves, 5 tablespoons of the vinegar, and 1.2 litres (2 pints) water in a large pan. Bring to the boil, then simmer for 20 minutes.
2. Add the skate to the simmering liquid and cook gently for about 15 minutes, until tender. Remove from the liquid and skin the fish. Keep warm on a serving dish.
3. Place the cream, capers, parsley, and salt and pepper in a pan and bring gently to simmering point. Simmer for 1 minute. Remove from the heat and stir in the remaining vinegar. Pour over the fish and garnish with parsley.

Serves 4
Preparation time:
15 minutes
Cooking time:
35 minutes
Freezing:
Not recommended

Illustrated on page 69

PLAITED TROUT WITH CREAMY TOMATO SAUCE

Less skilled cooks may find the filleting and skinning of the trout tricky and time-consuming. Follow the instructions on page 7 or ask at the fish counter for it to be done. The recipe is then very straightforward.

2 pink-fleshed trout, filleted and skinned
2 white-fleshed trout, filleted and skinned
6 tablespoons dry white wine
350 g (12 oz) ripe tomatoes, skinned
1 teaspoon tomato purée
2 teaspoons chopped chervil or parsley
2 tablespoons double cream
salt and pepper to taste
chervil sprigs and lemon slices to garnish

Serves 4
Preparation time:
25–30 minutes
Cooking time:
15 minutes
Freezing:
Not recommended

1. Cut each trout fillet lengthways into 3 strips. Plait 3 strips together using alternate white and pink flesh; half will have 2 white and 1 pink strip and the remainder will be the reverse.
2. Carefully place the plaits on a large buttered ovenproof dish, in one layer. Sprinkle with salt and pepper and half of the wine, cover tightly with foil and cook in a preheated oven, 200°C/400°F/Gas Mark 6, for 15 minutes.
3. Meanwhile, make the sauce. Cut the tomatoes into quarters and remove the seeds and cores. Chop the flesh finely and reserve half of it. Place the rest in a small pan with the seeds, cores, tomato purée and remaining wine. Bring to the boil, then simmer for 5 minutes, until reduced a little. Press through a sieve and return to the pan with the reserved tomato, herbs, cream, and salt and pepper. Reheat gently.
4. To serve, spoon the creamy tomato sauce onto 4 individual warmed plates. Place 2 trout plaits on top and garnish with chervil and lemon slices. Serve immediately with tiny new potatoes or rice pilaff.

Illustrated top right:
Carteret Skate
(page 67)

HALIBUT STEAKS WITH LEEK SAUCE

4 halibut or cod steaks, each weighing about 175 g (6 oz)
2 shallots or small onions, chopped
4 tablespoons dry white wine
25 g (1 oz) butter
2 leeks, sliced thinly
1 teaspoon chopped parsley
142 ml (5 fl oz) carton single cream
salt and pepper to taste

Serves 4
Preparation time:
15 minutes
Cooking time:
12–15 minutes
Freezing:
Not recommended

1. Place the halibut or cod in a buttered shallow dish in one layer. Sprinkle over the shallots or onions, wine, and salt and pepper. Cover with greaseproof paper and cook in a preheated oven, 180°C/350°F/Gas Mark 4, for 12–15 minutes, until tender. Transfer to a warmed serving dish with a fish slice and keep warm; strain the cooking liquor and set aside.
2. Melt the butter in a small pan, add the leeks and fry gently for 2 minutes. Add the reserved liquor and bring to the boil, then simmer for 2 minutes. Add the parsley and cream and heat through gently. Check the seasoning.
3. Serve the fish steaks with the sauce and courgettes.

TEMPURA

Tempura consists of morsels of fish and vegetables, coated in a light batter and deep-fried to perfect crispness. Have your guests seated while the food is cooking as it should be served piping hot.

12–16 raw Mediterranean prawns, peeled but with tails left on
175 g (6 oz) courgettes, sliced diagonally
125 g (4 oz) button mushrooms
1 red pepper, cored, seeded and cut into strips
1 small aubergine, sliced
1 onion, sliced into rings
oil for deep-frying
FOR THE BATTER:
50 g (2 oz) self-raising flour
50 g (2 oz) cornflour
½ teaspoon baking powder
1 egg, beaten
225 ml (7 fl oz) iced water (approximately)
salt to taste
TO SERVE:
150 ml (¼ pint) chicken stock
2 tablespoons light soy sauce
2 tablespoons dry sherry or sake
1 carrot, grated
1 turnip, grated

1. First make the batter. Sift the flour, cornflour, baking powder and salt into a bowl. Make a well in the centre and add the egg and a little water. Beat to incorporate the dry ingredients gradually, adding more water until a smooth light batter is formed.
2. Gently heat together the stock, soy sauce and sherry or sake and keep warm.
3. Cut each prawn down the back and remove the black intestine. Dip the prawns and vegetables in the batter, then deep-fry in batches; lower into hot oil and fry for about 2 minutes, until golden. Drain on kitchen paper; keep warm.
4. Place the warm liquid in 4 individual warmed bowls and sprinkle with the carrot and turnip. Dip the battered morsels into the sauce before eating.

Serves 4
Preparation time:
35 minutes
Cooking time:
2 minutes per batch
Freezing:
Not recommended

SALMON IN AN OVERCOAT

1 kg (2 lb) salmon tail, or salmon trout, filleted and skinned
50 g (2 oz) butter
1 teaspoon grated lemon rind
2 teaspoons chopped tarragon
1 tablespoon chopped parsley
500 g (1 lb) ready-made puff pastry
salt and pepper to taste
beaten egg to glaze
dill sprigs to garnish

Serves 4–6
Preparation time: 30 minutes
Cooking time: 35–40 minutes
Freezing: Recommended at end of stage 3

1. Season the salmon with salt and pepper. Beat together the butter, lemon rind and herbs.
2. Roll out half of the pastry on a lightly floured board to 2.5 cm (1 inch) larger all round than the fish. Place on a dampened baking sheet and place one fish fillet in the centre. Spread with the herb butter and place the second fish fillet on top. Brush the pastry edges with beaten egg.
3. Roll out the remaining pastry and use to cover the fish. Press the edges to seal, trim off excess pastry, then flute. Mark 'fish scales' with a teaspoon. Use the pastry trimmings to make the eye and fins. Brush with beaten egg.
4. Bake in a preheated oven, 220°C/425°F/Gas Mark 7, for 20 minutes, then lower the temperature to 160°C/325°F/Gas Mark 3, and cook for 15–20 minutes, until the pastry is golden and the fish is tender.
5. Transfer to a warmed serving platter and serve hot, garnished with dill.

SALMON AND WILD MUSHROOM PUFF PIES

250 g (8 oz) ready-made puff pastry
1 salmon fillet, weighing about 500 g (1 lb), skinned and cut into 4 pieces
25 g (1 oz) butter
125 g (4 oz) wild or cup mushrooms, sliced
1 teaspoon chopped tarragon
1 tablespoon snipped chives
2 teaspoons lemon juice
beaten egg to glaze
FOR THE SAUCE:
25 g (1 oz) butter
50 g (2 oz) watercress, chopped finely
142 ml (5 fl oz) carton single cream
1 teaspoon cornflour
½ teaspoon grated orange rind
salt and pepper to taste
TO GARNISH:
orange slices
few chives

1. Roll out the pastry on a floured surface and cut into eight 10 cm (4 inch) squares. Place 4 squares on a dampened baking sheet and place a piece of salmon on each.
2. Melt the butter in a small pan, add the mushrooms and cook gently for 5 minutes, until softened. Add the herbs, lemon juice, and salt and pepper and cook for 2 minutes. Cool slightly, then place on top of the salmon.
3. Brush the pastry edges with egg, place the remaining pastry squares on top, seal well, then flake the edge with a knife and flute. Mark a cross in the top of each pie.
4. Bake in a preheated oven, 200°C/400°F/Gas Mark 6, for 25–30 minutes, until well risen and golden brown.
5. Meanwhile, make the sauce. Melt the butter in a small pan, add the watercress and fry gently for 1 minute. Blend the cream with the cornflour and add to the pan with the orange rind, and salt and pepper. Bring gently to simmering point and cook for 2 minutes.
6. Transfer the pies to individual warmed plates and pour the sauce around them. Garnish with orange and chives.

Serves 4
Preparation time:
35 minutes
Cooking time:
25–30 minutes
Freezing:
Recommended at end of stage 3

MEDITERRANEAN BAKED BASS

1 sea bass, weighing 1 kg (2 lb), gutted and scaled
2 teaspoons chopped thyme
1 tablespoon each chopped oregano, parsley and marjoram
2 tablespoons olive oil
1 onion, chopped
2 cloves garlic, chopped
3 Beefsteak tomatoes, skinned and sliced
125 g (4 oz) black olives
1 green pepper, cored, seeded and sliced into rings
150 ml (1/4 pint) dry white wine
sea salt and pepper to taste

Serves 6–8
Preparation time: 30 minutes
Cooking time: 30–40 minutes
Freezing: Not recommended

1. Season the fish inside and out with sea salt and pepper. Mix together the herbs and sprinkle some inside the fish.
2. Drizzle half of the oil over the base of a baking dish large enough to take the fish. Sprinkle with half of the onion, 1 clove garlic and half of the remaining herb mixture. Place the fish on top.
3. Arrange the tomato slices over the fish and sprinkle with the remaining onion, garlic and herbs. Scatter the olives and green pepper over the top, pour over the wine and season with sea salt and pepper.
4. Cook in a preheated oven, 200°C/400°F/Gas Mark 6, for 30–40 minutes, basting with the juices two or three times during cooking.
5. To serve, cut down the centre of the fish and lift out portions with a spatula. Serve with warm crusty bread or potatoes.

KING PRAWNS CREOLE

This is a useful dish for entertaining as it can be made completely in advance and simply reheated for serving. A rice pilaff is just right with it, plus a green salad containing avocado and watercress.

1 kg (2 lb) raw headless prawns
150 ml (1/4 pint) dry white wine
few peppercorns
celery leaves
bouquet garni
2 tablespoons oil
1 onion, chopped finely
2 cloves garlic, chopped
1 tablespoon paprika
1 teaspoon ground coriander
1 teaspoon ground cumin
500 g (1 lb) ripe tomatoes, skinned and chopped
2 teaspoons tomato purée
salt and pepper to taste
1 tablespoon chopped coriander to garnish

1. Peel the prawns, reserving the shells, and cut down the backs to remove the black intestine. Wash and dry the prawns and set aside. Wash the shells and place in a pan with the wine, peppercorns, celery leaves and bouquet garni. Bring to the boil, then cover and simmer for 30 minutes. Strain and set aside.
2. Heat the oil in a saucepan, add the prawns and fry quickly, stirring, for 3–5 minutes, until they turn pink. Remove with a slotted spoon and drain on kitchen paper.
3. Add the onion and garlic to the pan and fry until softened. Stir in the paprika, ground coriander and cumin and cook for 1 minute. Add the tomatoes, tomato purée, reserved stock, and salt and pepper and bring to the boil. Simmer, uncovered, for 15 minutes, until slightly thickened. Add the prawns and simmer for 5 minutes.
4. Sprinkle with the chopped coriander to serve.

Serves 4
Preparation time:
45 minutes
Cooking time:
About 25 minutes
Freezing:
Recommended

BASS WRAPPED IN LETTUCE

Serve this beautiful dish of bass in a lettuce overcoat as the centrepiece for a special dinner. Follow the instructions on page 7 or ask at the fish counter for the fish to be filleted and skinned, to give you 2 large fillets.

25 g (1 oz) butter
2 shallots or 1 onion, chopped finely
1 crisp lettuce, e.g. Iceberg
125 g (4 oz) spinach
2 tablespoons chopped mixed herbs, e.g. tarragon, chives, chervil, mint
1 tablespoon lemon juice
1 sea bass, weighing about 1.25 kg (2½ lb), filleted and skinned
150 ml (¼ pint) dry white wine
2 tablespoons dry vermouth (optional)
4 tablespoons double cream
salt and pepper to taste

Serves 6
Preparation time:
35 minutes
Cooking time:
30–40 minutes
Freezing:
Not recommended

1. Melt the butter in a small pan, add half of the shallots or onion and fry gently until softened; set aside.
2. Blanch the lettuce quickly in a pan of boiling salted water; drain well in a colander. Set aside 12–14 leaves; chop the rest very finely.
3. Place the spinach, with just the water clinging to the leaves after washing, in a pan, cover and cook for about 5 minutes, until tender. Drain well, pressing out as much liquid as possible. Chop very finely.
4. Mix together the chopped lettuce, spinach, fried shallot or onion, herbs, lemon juice, and salt and pepper.
5. Place 6–7 lettuce leaves along a buttered baking dish large enough to take the fish. Place 1 fish fillet on the leaves, sprinkle with salt and pepper, then spread the spinach mixture evenly over the top. Cover with the other fish fillet and sprinkle with salt and pepper. Place the remaining lettuce over the fish, wrapping around to enclose it completely. Sprinkle over the remaining shallot or onion, wine and vermouth, if using, and cover with buttered greaseproof paper.
6. Cook in a preheated oven, 180°C/350°F/Gas Mark 4, for 30–40 minutes, until tender. Carefully transfer the fish with a fish slice to a warmed serving plate and keep warm while preparing the sauce; reserve the cooking liquor.
7. Strain the reserved liquor into a small pan and boil quickly until reduced by half. Lower the heat and stir in the cream. Check the seasoning.
8. Cut the fish into slices to serve and pour a little sauce over each portion. Serve with carrots and courgettes.

Illustrated bottom: Janice's Scobeche (page 78)

JANICE'S SCOBECHE

This fiery Jamaican recipe was given to me by a friend, whose family is from the Caribbean. If you can take your food very hot, use the Jamaican chilli peppers called Scotch bonnet—it is advisable to wear rubber gloves when handling them.

1 kg (2 lb) red snapper, gutted and scaled
2 tablespoons lime juice
4 tablespoons oil
2 onions, sliced thinly
2 red chillies, chopped
2 Beefsteak tomatoes, skinned and chopped
4 tablespoons red wine vinegar
salt and pepper to taste
herb sprigs to garnish

Serves 4–6
Preparation time: 20 minutes, plus standing time
Cooking time: 35–40 minutes
Freezing: Recommended

Illustrated on page 77

1. Sprinkle the fish inside and out with the lime juice, and salt and pepper. Leave for 10 minutes.
2. Pour half of the oil into a roasting tin large enough to take the fish snugly. Place it in a preheated oven, 190°C/375°F/Gas Mark 5, for about 5 minutes until hot. Add the fish, baste with the hot oil and cook for 35–40 minutes, until tender.
3. Meanwhile, make the marinade. Heat the remaining oil in a saucepan, add the onions and fry until softened and browned. Add the chillies, tomatoes, vinegar, and salt and pepper, bring to the boil, then simmer for 5 minutes.
4. Transfer the fish to a warmed serving dish and pour over the hot marinade. Leave for 10 minutes and serve warm garnished with herbs, or leave until cold. To portion the fish, cut it down the centre and remove the flesh from the bones with a spatula.

FRUITS DE MER GLACÉS

The ice bowl container for the seafood is very easy to make and looks spectacular. Remember to place it on a lipped plate as it will start to melt after about 1 hour.

chervil, mint, dill and rosemary sprigs
cucumber slices
lemon and lime slices
12 oysters (optional)
few pink peppercorns (optional)
8 cooked langoustines or Mediterranean prawns
500–750 g (1–1½ lb) cooked prawns in shell
4–6 cooked crab claws
TO GARNISH:
lemon and lime slices
herb sprigs

1. Pour 1.2 litres (2 pints) water into a 2.25 litre (4 pint) plastic pudding basin. Place a 1.2 litre (2 pint) plastic basin in the centre and fill it with weights until the top is level with the top of the larger bowl. Place sticky tape across the bowls to keep the smaller one centred. Fill up with water if necessary to within 2.5 cm (1 inch) of the top.
2. Place herb sprigs, cucumber, lemon and lime slices in the water. Carefully place in the freezer overnight, until completely frozen.
3. When ready to serve, remove the sticky tape, pour hot water around the inside bowl to loosen it, then remove the bowl. Wrap hot towels around the outside bowl to loosen, then remove it.
4. Place the ice bowl on a large serving platter and arrange cracked ice around it. Place the oysters on the cracked ice and sprinkle with the peppercorns, if using. Fill the bowl with the remaining shellfish, draping the langoustines or Mediterranean prawns over the edge.
5. Garnish with lemon, lime and herbs. Serve with brown bread and mayonnaise flavoured with chopped herbs.

Serves 4–6
Preparation time:
15 minutes, plus freezing time

INDEX

Photography by: Charlie Stebbings
Designed by: Sue Storey
Home economist: Mary Cadogan
Stylist: Penny Legg
Illustration by: Linda Smith
Line drawings by: Lily Whitlock
Typeset by Rowland Phototypesetting Limited